The Great Book of Asian American Heroes

18 Asian American Men and Women
Who Changed American History

Bill O'Neill

DON'T FORGET YOUR FREE BOOKS

CONTENTS

INTRODUCTION

When it comes to those who have contributed to American history, most people tend to think in black and white, forgetting that plenty of people of Asian descent are also generational or heritage Americans. Yes, Asian-Americans have been part of the American story for quite some time and they've contributed to it in many ways. In *The Great Book of Asian-American Heroes*, you'll read about 18 men and women of Asian descent who've made significant impacts in the Asian-American communities they came from, as well as greater American society.

Each chapter covers one hero and generally follows their life story, focusing on what made that person famous or important. Each chapter ends with a "Did You Know?" section of five interesting facts about the person.

You probably already know a few things about some notable Asian-Americans, but this book will bring your knowledge to a whole new level in a fun and engaging way. Most of our heroes are of Chinese and Japanese descent, but our heroes also include people of southeast Asian, Polynesian, and even Indian descent.

From entertainers such as Pat Morita and Henry Cho to scientists like Michio Kaku and Har Gobind Khorana, and athletes such as Bruce Lee and Kristi Yamaguchi, we have it covered.

This book also profiles some of the most important Asian-American politicians, artists, and entrepreneurs in history. Furthermore, two of the chapters profile collective groups of Asian-American heroes who helped build and fight for the US, although their efforts have often been overlooked.

So, sit back, relax, and embark on an amazing journey through nearly 200 years of Asian-American success stories. These men and women prove that when it comes to contributing to their country, they are truly imbued with the American spirit.

CHAPTER 1

Haing S. Ngor: Surviving the Killing Fields

Most people today live pretty boring lives. We work, start families, retire, and die. That's not to say that we don't have a lot of fun between point A and point B, or that we don't do anything important - raising children is one of the most important things in the world - but most of our lives are pretty predictable.

If we're lucky, we choose to attend a certain college and study a specific subject.

We focus our energies on landing work in a certain profession.

And we are attracted to a certain person that becomes our partner.

But not everyone has the luxury of stability and predictability. Some people's lives are in constant flux to the point of chaos, and yet, they still manage to be successful and even influential.

Cambodian-born American actor Haing S. Ngor was one such person.

Ngor was an ambitious and bright young man who did all the right things, but none of it mattered after a brutal dictator came to power in his country, ruining his and millions of other people's lives in the process. After losing everything, Ngor made his way to the United States where he started over again from the bottom.

Thanks to a quintessential "lucky break" while he was in Tinseltown, Ngor got a role in the 1984 film *The Killing Fields*, which was about the dictatorship of Pol Pot in Cambodia. Ngor's riveting portrayal of a man who had lost everything, and who was essentially powerless in the face of unspeakable cruelty and violence, earned him an Oscar Award for best-supporting actor. He was the first and presently is the only Asian actor to have won the award.

Ngor then settled into a comfortable, predictable life that most thought he had earned and was owed, but then in a tragic turn of irony, he was murdered on the streets of Los Angeles.

FROM DOCTOR TO SURVIVOR

Haing Somnang Ngor was born on March 22, 1940, in French Indochina, which would later become Cambodia. Ngor worked hard, went to medical school, and by the mid-1970s, he was a successful gynecologist in Cambodia's capital city of Phnom Penh. Ngor married and was about to welcome his first child into the family when his life took its first major turn.

In 1975, the Khmer Rouge took over Cambodia and refashioned it into a communist dictatorship known as Democratic Kampuchea.

Overnight the perfect, seemingly idyllic yet boring life that Ngor had known was over. He was immediately thrust into a place and way of life to which he wasn't accustomed. Ngor quickly found out that the medical degrees he had hanging on his wall and most of what he had learned at university and medical school were worthless.

Nothing could have prepared Ngor for the four years of hell he experienced in Cambodia's notorious "killing fields."

The Khmer Rouge, which was led by Pol Pot, proved to be one of the most brutal and unpredictable dictatorships in modern history. After the Khmer Rouge took over the country, they depopulated most of the major cities, sending the hated urbanites to the country to work in the rice fields.

Those who were known to be educated - or even those who simply wore glasses - were worked extra hard and given fewer rations.

Some were just outright executed.

Ngor kept his background a secret, telling police and soldiers that he was a cab driver. But when his pregnant wife was about to give birth, Ngor was faced with yet another major twist in his life.

Ngor knew his wife needed a Caesarian section to save her and the baby's lives, and he knew how to do the operation since he was a gynecologist. However, doing so in the concentration camp would've meant exposing his background.

He tried to successfully deliver the baby without a Caesarian section, but he was unsuccessful; both his wife and child died.

Needless to say, it was a choice that hopefully none of us has to make. As we live our boring, ordinary lives, more than likely none of us will even have to consider such a choice, but for Haing Ngor, it was a matter of survival.

The choice Ngor made bothered him throughout his entire life—he never remarried and never had any more children. He pointed this out on more than one occasion after he became successful, telling reporters, "[No matter] How rich you are, you can't buy a happy family."

But Haing Ngor was a resilient man, who despite immense loss and suffering, made it his life's mission to make something positive out of what he, his family, and his countrymen suffered in the killing fields.

A CHANCE FOR REDEMPTION

Like all brutal totalitarian regimes, the Khmer Rouge didn't last long, falling in 1979 under the pressures of international opposition and its own destructive nature that all but destroyed Cambodia's economy and infrastructure. For most Cambodians, including Haing Ngor, this was welcome news. It meant a chance at having a normal life. However, it also meant that more struggles were ahead.

For Ngor, he saw it as an opportunity to deal with the guilt and shame over the death of his wife and to redeem himself and his people.

After the collapse of the Khmer Rouge, Haing and his niece Sophia Ngor lived for several months in refugee camps in Thailand. He used his medical training to help people in the camps and he began writing down some of his painful memories of the killing fields.

In August 1980, Ngor received the first good news in as long as he could remember when he was notified by the US State Department that his asylum application had been granted. And to make things even better, his niece's application had also been accepted. Haing and Sophia left for Southern California where they had support from members of the Cambodian community.

Unfortunately for Haing, though, he was never licensed to practice medicine in the US so he had to find other work.

The amiable Ngor put his experiences and personality to use helping Southeast Asian refugees in Southern California, which is where he was "discovered" by casting directors working on the 1984 feature film, *The Killing Fields*.

The Killing Fields, which was a critical and box office hit, stars Sam Watterson as an American journalist and Haing Ngor as his friend and colleague, Cambodian journalist Dith Pran. The film follows Pran's brutal saga through Pol Pot's regime, as he loses everything.

The character of Dith Pran reflected Haing Ngor's troubled life in so many ways.

But beyond the depravities that the character of Dith Pran and the real Haing Ngor suffered in Cambodia, both also eventually found redemption.

The Killing Fields brought Haing Ngor professional success in the form of a coveted Oscar award and more film roles. Ngor's acting career also brought him financial success, which he used to support clinics in his native Cambodia.

"He had a largeness of heart that was all-encompassing," said actor friend Matt Salinger of Ngor's generosity.

By the 1990s, Ngor had become an American citizen and continued to act and support the Cambodian community. After a lifetime of turmoil, Ngor had finally built the fairly stable - and in many ways, boring - sort of life that we all take for granted.

But on February 25, 1996, it all came to a tragic end when Ngor was shot and killed in an apparent robbery gone wrong outside his Los Angeles home in the Chinatown neighborhood.

The police and prosecutors later established that the three men who killed Ngor were members of an Asian street gang. They were attempting to take his Rolex watch and a locket belonging to his late wife when the deadly struggle ensued.

If only they'd known who Haing Ngor was and what he had been through. Maybe things would've turned out differently.

DID YOU KNOW?

- Haing parlayed his fame from *The Killing Fields* into a successful career as a writer. In 1988, his book *Hain Ngor: A Cambodian Odyssey*, which tells of his struggle to survive during Pol Pot's regime, was released. The book was a hit and a new edition was published as *Survival in the Killing Fields*.

- Ngor's late wife's name was My-Huoy.

- Ngor spent most of his time in traditional-style prisons instead of the notorious killing fields, which is where the Khmer Rouge's most despised enemies were sent. However, just as Dith Pran traveled through the jungle to a Red Cross camp in the film, so too did Ngor in real life.

- After Ngor was murdered, many in southern California's Cambodian community made claims on his wealth, including one woman who said she was his wife. His younger brother got most of his assets in Cambodia, while lawyers received the bulk of Ngor's American wealth, fighting off illegitimate claims.

- Although Ngor's killers were known members of a gang, and all had criminal records, their defense lawyers argued, with no supporting evidence, that the murder was a Khmer Rouge revenge assassination. In a final ironic twist to a life that was full of many twists, the three killers were convicted on April 16, 1998, which also happened to be the day that dictator Pol Pot's death was announced.

CHAPER 2

Maya Lin: Memorializing Those Who Gave All

Like most people, Americans proudly build and showcase memorials to their heroes. Many of the heroes are presidents, more than a few are military-related, while others include scientists, philosophers, and other people who have made significant contributions to American history.

Some of these monuments, like the Washington Monument or the Lincoln Memorial, have become so well-known that even if you've never visited any of them, you certainly know what they look like.

These monuments were so well-built that they have become an enduring part of the fabric of American culture. And as history continues to be made, new monuments are erected to memorialize the contributions that men and women have made to the process.

In 1982, the Vietnam Veterans Memorial monument was built in Washington, D.C. to memorialize the 58,320 names of Americans who died in the Vietnam War. It was a monument that many thought - was a long time coming, but the Vietnam War had divided the country, and it was only beginning to heal by the early 1980s.

So, in 1981, the federal government announced that it would have a national competition to decide the design of the Vietnam Veterans Memorial. Out of the 1,422 submissions, 21-year-old Maya Lin's was chosen as the winner.

It was truly a phenomenal achievement for Lin and the Asian-American community, many of whom saw it as their acceptance into American society.

AMERICAN BORN AND RAISED

Although Maya Lin was born to Chinese born and raised parents, her life began in Athens, Ohio in 1959. In case you don't know, Athens is located in the heart of Ohio, which is in the heart of America.

You can't get any more American than Athens, Ohio.

And that's how Maya Lin saw herself as she grew up, even stating in an interview that she "basically didn't even realize I was Chinese," until she got older, adding, "I was a kid from Ohio."

Lin would later develop an interest in Chinese and Asian architecture, but during her formative years, she focused on learning the foundations of design and architecture and doing well in school.

Like many Asian-American parents, Maya's—Henry and Julia—pushed her to excel academically, although Maya truly enjoyed books, learning, and school and didn't need to be prodded very much. Lin's hard work gained her admission into Yale, where she earned a BA in 1981 and an MA in architecture in 1986.

While studying at Yale, Lin developed her own unique, post-modern architectural style that focuses on how the image she is creating interacts with the environment around it. Lin did well in her classes and dedicated most of her time to her studies, as she had in high school. However, she was still very cognizant of the changes that were taking place in the United States.

In 1980, America elected Ronald Reagan, who led the country on a different path. Under Reagan, patriotism was cool again and those who died fighting for their country were to be given places of honor.

DESIGNING THE WALL

When Ronald Reagan came into office in 1981, the United States was experiencing a minor cultural shift. Most Americans were tired of the counter-culture chaos of the 1960s and '70s; many of those who had participated in it as hippies were even becoming yuppies by the '80s. The US had definitely become a bit more culturally and politically conservative, and with that turn came a new respect for some traditions.

Traditions such as honoring veterans.

The Vietnam War may not have been the costliest American war in terms of lives lost, but it was perhaps the most polarizing conflict since the Civil War. Families were divided over support or opposition to the war, so when it finally ended in 1975, many Americans wanted to forget about it.

And forget about it they did until Reagan came into office.

The Reaganism of the '80s was a conservative philosophy that wanted to uphold the men and women who fought in America's wars. It also didn't hurt that the baby boomers who fought in Vietnam were by then voting and were also becoming part of the power structure.

So, in early 1981, the government decided to commission a contest to decide the design of the monument. At stake was $20,000, but even more important was the prestige of having your name associated with a piece of American history.

More than 2,000 people registered for the initial competition but only 1,421 officially submitted designs. Among them was an unknown designer/architect named Maya Lin.

As Lin took a vigorous course load at Yale, she heard about the contest and decided to give it a try. Although she was confident in her abilities, she knew she was up against some pretty stiff competition.

Lin's design comprises two, 246-foot and 9-inch-long black granite walls that are divided into 140 panels. The apex where the panels meet is just over ten feet tall. From the middle, both walls gradually taper until they are just eight inches on either end.

The walls were to be built into the ground. As Lin later said, the Memorial was to resemble "a wound in the earth that is slowly healing."

The focal point of the monument was the names of every serviceman, and eight women, who died in the Vietnam War inscribed on the panels.

Lin submitted her blind entry as contestant #1026. In May 1981, a Marine colonel came to Lin's dorm room to announce that she had won the contest.

Of course, not everyone liked her decidedly post-modern style and more than a few people thought that someone of Asian ancestry shouldn't have been allowed to even enter the competition.

But not long after the Vietnam Veterans Memorial opened to the public in 1982, it became clear to everyone how poignant it is.

If you've ever been to the Vietnam Veterans Memorial, or even to one of the portable, smaller versions known as "The Moving Wall," then you know how powerful the experience is. It was a war that most Americans still have a difficult time understanding, but the feelings that the monument brings out in those who view it have universal appeal. Seeing those names on the panels that stretch on and on invokes quite the emotion, which is accentuated by Lin's post-modern design style.

A traditional neo-classical style of architecture just couldn't have captured the feeling of this modern war that so few understood.

Lin went on to have a successful career in design and architecture, designing the Civil Rights Memorial in Montgomery, Alabama as well as numerous other buildings and works of art. When asked about her influences, Lin has said that they come from a combination of Middle America and China, stating:

"Obviously, for me home is Athens, Ohio, in America, but at the same time, in my 20s and 30s, I realized how much my aesthetic is influenced by my parents' aesthetics. And how much were they influenced by the fact that they were born and raised in Shanghai and Beijing?"

Today, millions of Americans of all backgrounds view Maya Lin as a true heroine for setting in stone the memories of those who gave their all in the Vietnam War.

DID YOU KNOW?

- The Vietnam Veterans' Memorial averages about 4.5 million visitors per year, with 5.6 million visiting in 2015. Due to the COVID-19 pandemic, only 1.59 million people visited it in 2020.

- President Obama awarded Lin the Presidential Medal of Freedom in 2016.

- One of the most noticeable elements of the Vietnam Veterans' Memorial is the three bronze soldier statues known as *The Three Soldiers*. Lin did not design this piece and was initially against having it installed in front of the memorial. A compromise was finally reached in 1984 where the statues would be placed to the side of the walls.

- Although the Vietnam Veterans' Memorial doesn't stylistically look much like most of the other monuments in Washington, one of its walls looks toward the Washington Monument and the other to the Lincoln Memorial, giving it a sense of symmetry and belonging in the monumental landscape.

- Lin was married to art photography dealer Daniel Wolf, who died of a heart attack in 2021 at the age of 65. Lin had two daughters with Wolf, India and Rachel.

CHAPTER 3

Pat Morita:
From Arnold to Mr. Miyagi

If you grew up in the 1970s or '80s, you no doubt remember seeing Noriyuki Morita on the small and big screens. Who is Noriyuki Morita, you're probably wondering?

How about Pat Morita? Or better yet, you probably remember Arnold, the Asian drive-in owner from *Happy Days*, right? And if you somehow don't remember that then you would definitely remember Morita playing Mr. Miyagi in the *Karate Kid* movies (we're talking about the original ones).

Yes, during the '70s and into the '80s, Morita was everywhere, showing his acting talents and versatility and that he was so much more than an "Asian actor."

True, the American-born actor of Japanese ancestry did play roles that focused on his Asian ancestry, but even his *Happy Days* character, which was certainly on the cheesy side, was not exploitative. Through his career, Pat Morita demonstrated that Asian-American actors could be funny or dramatic, in their own right, and not just for being Asian.

Thanks to Morita's efforts in the '70s and '80s, he opened the doors in television and film for later actors of Asian ancestry to play roles that depended more on their experience and talents and less on their ethnicity.

A ROUGH START

Noriyuki "Pat" Morita was born in 1932 in the Sacramento, California area to Japanese immigrant parents. His early family life was fairly stable economically, with both parents working and in the house, but other elements of his youth were quite chaotic.

And most of the chaos was out of Morita's control.

Morita suffered from spinal tuberculosis from the age of two until he was 11, spending most of that time in hospitals. When young Morita wasn't having surgery on his back, he was confined to a full-body cast, unable to do the things that other kids his age enjoyed.

The situation led Morita to look inward and find his voice. He was an exceptionally bright young boy and was especially well-spoken, which often bemused generational Americans that he met who expected him to speak with a heavy Asian accent.

No - by 1943, Pat Morita was a typical American boy in most ways. His medical issues slowed him down, but they didn't prevent him from joking about his situation, or the situation of Asian- Americans in general. Young Pat Morita was a comedic hit with his family and anyone who met him, but unfortunately for him and nearly every person of Japanese ancestry living on the West Coast, 1943 proved to be a bad year.

When the Japanese bombed Pearl Harbor, Hawaii on December 7, 1941, it led to the United States declaring war on Japan, the Axis Powers declaring war on the US, and Americans mobilizing for war.

One of the first, and most controversial things American President Franklin Roosevelt did was signing Executive Order 9066 on February 12, 1942. It ordered more than 112,000 people of Japanese ancestry, including generational Americans, out of the West Coast and into internment camps. Among them were Morita's family - but not Morita, who was in the hospital.

When Morita was finally released from the hospital in 1943, he was sent to live with his family in internment camps in Arizona and California.

Needless to say, living in the internment camps was a tough experience. However, the Morita family stayed together and when the war ended, they returned to Sacramento to run a Chinese restaurant. Yes, you read that right - the Japanese Morita family ran a Chinese restaurant in a racially mixed neighborhood of Sacramento. The fact is that, after World War II, the Japanese were still viewed by many Americans negatively, and Chinese cuisine had a much older history in the US, so it was a sound business decision by the Morita's.

The situation would later provide grist for Morita's career as a standup comedian and inspiration for some of his acting roles. It also wouldn't be the last time Morita played the part of a Chinese person.

Morita was hit with one final tragedy in his youth when his father, Tamaru, was killed by a hit-and-run driver in 1956.

The death of the Morita patriarch shook the family, and although Pat continued to run the family restaurant with his mother Momoe, it was soon time for him to move on.

MAKING IT BIG

As was expected of him, Pat Morita was a good son to his parents. He married a Japanese-American woman in 1953 and started a family. Morita worked several jobs in the '50s and '60s and became quite successful in California's booming aerospace industry.

But no matter where Morita went, or whatever he did, he was always cracking jokes and making people smile. People told him he should try his luck in standup comedy, and after he did a small gig at a Sacramento nightclub, he was hooked.

Morita took the name "Pat" but kept his last name to emphasize both his Asian and American heritage. And that's the type of set that Morita did and became known for around northern California: he was an American who understood American humor and comedic timing, but he offered a different perspective as someone of Japanese ancestry.

The small clubs of northern California weren't the place to make it big, though, so Morita took other comedians' advice by taking his act to the Los Angeles area.

Not long after arriving in Tinseltown, things changed quickly for the small-town boy.

He found the Hollywood lifestyle to his liking, but it came at the expense of developing a drinking problem, and it cost him his first marriage.

But by the late 1960s, he was also getting noticed by some pretty important people.

Redd Foxx, who was already legendary at that time, took Morita under his wing and mentored him on the entertainment industry and life in general. Morita opened up for Foxx's act, which in turn, opened many professional doors for him.

Eventually, Morita saw Foxx as his "godfather," giving him life as well as comedy lessons.

Morita recalled in a later interview, in a very good Redd Foxx voice, how he once went to Foxx for some money to buy a house:

"You wanna pay me back, I know you're gonna make it one day, son…You do this for somebody else."

Morita said that he always remembered that and would later pay Foxx back by financially helping many struggling actors.

By the early 1970s, though, Morita didn't need to go to Foxx or anyone else for money. He began landing supporting roles regularly in television, most notably as Sam Pak on *M*A*S*H*, Arnold on *Happy Days*, and Ah Chew on Redd Foxx's *Sanford and Son*.

There were also a couple of flops sandwiched in there like *Mr. T and Tina* and *Blansky's Beauties*, but it was an otherwise successful career, more so than any other Asian-American of the era and arguably of all time.

Morita even played a dramatic role as a World War II Japanese naval officer in the 1976 epic film *Midway*.

But if you were a kid in the '80s, there's no doubt you remember Pat Morita best as Mr. Miyagi.

In the 1984 film *The Karate Kid*, Morita combined his comedic background with his, for the most part untapped, dramatic abilities to give life to the character of Mr. Miyagi, a lonely Japanese American martial arts master who mentors the main character on karate and life.

America fell in love with Mr. Miyagi and in many ways, he stole the show. The role saw Morita nominated for an Oscar for best supporting actor, but if you'll remember, Asian-American actor Hiang S. Ngor won the award that year.

Morita would go on to play Mr. Miyagi in three more *Karate Kid* films (yes, there were actually four, but we all try to forget about that last one!), eventually becoming one with the role. In many ways, it's how he's best remembered.

Pat Morita died in 2005 at the age of 73, but he left a powerful, lasting legacy. Morita broke down barriers and set the tone for Asian-American actors and comedians in the decades after he made it big and he produced some really good work that everyone can enjoy.

DID YOU KNOW?

- Pat Morita was married three times. He had one daughter, Erin, with his first wife, Kathleen Yamachi. He had two daughters, Aly and Tia, with his second wife, Yukiye Kitahara. He married Evelyn Guerrero in 1994 and remained married to her until he died.

- Despite being associated with martial arts through his characters of Arnold and Mr. Miyagi, Morita wasn't skilled in karate and only learned enough for his roles.

- Although Aly Morita believes that Pat was typecast after *The Karate Kid*, he did appear in 100 more roles after the first film in the franchise.

- Morita appeared on the country-themed variety talk show, *Glen Campbell Goodtime Hour* in 1968, doing a standup routine as "The Hip Nip" (a moniker playing on a common ethnic slur of the time).

- In 2021, the documentary, *More Than Miyagi: The Pat Morita Story* was released, giving fans an in-depth look into the actor and comedian's life. According to the film, Morita battled alcoholism for most of his adult life, which may have contributed to his health problems.

CHAPER 4

Wally Yonamine: Breaking Sports Barriers

You've probably heard the saying that there's nothing more American than baseball and apple pie, right? Well, you could also say that there's nothing more Japanese than baseball and sushi.

When Japan opened to the world in 1868 and ushered in what is known as the Meiji Era, the country rapidly transformed into a modern industrial, economic, and military power. The speed of Japan's modernization was amazing and nothing short of a miracle, and perhaps just as amazing is how the Japanese were able to balance their centuries-old cultural traditions with the new influences from the outside world.

One outside influence that the Japanese quickly adopted was the very American sport of baseball.

Professional leagues formed in Japan and during the decades before World War II, a few Americans who were up and coming - or at the end of their careers - even tried their luck in the Land of the Rising Sun. But World War II put a temporary end to the cultural exchanges.

The war also damaged relations between the Japanese and the Americans, sowing distrust in a generation of people from both nations.

But as Japanese and Japanese-Americans were being released from internment camps after World War II, and as the Japanese were cleaning up their bombed-out cities, an American Nisei (second-generation Japanese American) did what he could to help the two countries heal.

Wally Yonamine may not be a household name, but he should be. The Hawaiian-born Japanese American athlete broke down many barriers and, in the process, helped Japan and the USA move on, even if just a little, from the devastation of World War II. Yonamine was the second Asian-American and the first Japanese-American to play professional football, but it was on the baseball diamond where he made the greatest impact.

After playing in the American minors for several years, Yonamine brought his skills to the burgeoning Japanese professional baseball leagues. He was the first American to play professionally in Japan after World War II, eventually becoming a fan favorite among the Japanese.

Yonamine changed many aspects of the way baseball was played in Japan, but perhaps most important was how he served as a symbol of peace and renewed friendship between the American and the Japanese peoples.

A NATURAL ATHLETE

Yonamine was born and raised on the island of Maui in what was then the Territory of Hawaii in 1925. Although Wally's parents, father Matsusai and mother Kikue, were Japanese born, they raised him to be 100% American.

Yonamine didn't learn Japanese until he moved to Japan as an adult and he was quick to point out that he never liked sushi and wasn't much of a fan of Japanese food in general.

It was clear to Matsusai that his young son was extremely athletically talented. It seemed like whatever sport he played - football, baseball, or basketball - he was successful. The elder Yonamine began to think his son's talents were being wasted on the less-populated island of Maui. He arranged for Wally to attend high school in Honolulu, where he could attract attention from universities and professional scouts.

Now, people back then generally didn't consider Asians as athletes, so the fact that Ohio State University offered a football scholarship to Yonamine was quite incredible, especially when you consider that World War II was raging.

But the war ultimately put a damper on Yonamine's dream to play college ball.

Upon graduating from high school in 1945, Yonamine was drafted into the Army. He thought he'd end up with the all-Nisei unit fighting in Italy at the time (we'll get to them later in this book), but as Yonamine later reminisced, things worked out differently....

"But then the war in Europe ended and then Japan surrendered. So, I spent two years at Schofield Barracks on Oahu, peeling potatoes and playing football and baseball."

For Yonamine, the war was much easier than it could have been in more than one way. First, since his family lived in Hawaii, they avoided the internment camps the Japanese and Japanese Americans living on the West Coast had to endure. Second, he was able to work on his athletic skills, which earned him the attention of the San Francisco 49ers.

The 49ers offered Yonamine a contract for the 1947 season, making him the second Asian-American and the first - and only – Japanese-American to play professional gridiron football.

But it wasn't meant to be. After a lackluster season and a serious injury to his wrist, Yonamine was released by the 49ers.

Yonamine, though, had learnt from his parents the very Japanese ethic of always looking ahead and never complaining, so he began working on his baseball skills. He then contacted a minor league baseball manager named Lefty O'Doul who got him a minor league contract.

Yonamine was an excellent defensive player and a good hitter for average, but there was one important thing missing in his game.

"By 1950 I was hitting .335 and playing center field pretty well. I was the No. 4 hitter in the league. But I wasn't hitting home runs, and I knew that would keep me out of the majors," said Yonamine about his minor league career.

So, O'Doul suggested Yonamine should try his hand in Japan. After all, Yonamine was Japanese so the transition should be easy, or so he thought.

NOT A WARM WELCOME

When Wally Yonamine arrived in Tokyo in 1951 to play for the Yomiuri Giants, Japan's oldest professional baseball team, he was treated well by the owners and management, with indifference from the other players, and with outright hostility by the fans.

Wally Yonamine may have looked Japanese, but to the average Japanese fan, who could still see the signs of destruction left by World War II daily, he was an American and therefore an enemy.

Some people have compared Yonamine's foray into Japanese professional baseball with that of Jackie Robinson in the Majors, but Yonamine himself was quick to point out that although the situations did have similarities, Robinson's was much more intense, to say the least.

"You can call me the Jackie Robinson of Japanese baseball only in the sense that I was a pioneer, the first American, but not really in the sense of the kind of discrimination that Robinson put up with," Yonamine said. "I mean, at first the fans over here threw stuff at me and yelled at me, but I never had to deal with anything like Robinson did."

The first couple of years in Japan were tough for Yonamine. He constantly found himself starving for hamburgers and hotdogs. Even if you could have found a restaurant with American food in 1950s Tokyo, Yonamine would have had a difficult time asking directions because his Japanese was quite limited.

Eventually, Yonamine's wife Jane was brought over to Japan so the Japanese-American phenomenon could focus on his game.

And focus he did, hitting .311 over a course of 12 years with two different teams. Yonamine also won three batting titles, was selected as an all-star seven times, and was the Nippon Professional Baseball League's MVP in 1957.

After his playing career was over, Yonamine went on to manage for 20 years.

But Wally Yonamine was a modest person who would never admit publicly that he was a barrier breaker.

Despite his modesty, it's clear that besides being the first American to play professional baseball in Japan after World War II, Yonamine brought a whole new style of the game to Japan.

Before Yonamine came to Japan, stealing bases was a rarity. Yonamine was taught how to play tough and slide through an infielder, if need be, which was a taboo in Japan in the 1950s.

"In Hawaii, I'd been taught as a kid that when you're the lead baserunner on a double-play ball, you knock down that second baseman and break it up. Well, the first few times I did that over here, people were shocked. It was something that just wasn't done. It was unsportsmanlike," Yonamine said.

Yonamine's rough base running was another factor in the Japanese fans' initial dislike of Yonamine, although they did come around. Wally Yonamine eventually became a well-liked and respected player and manager in Japan, becoming the first American to be inducted into the Japanese Baseball Hall of Fame in 1994.

Wally Yonamine's rough American style of play gradually caught on in Japan and later Korea, but most important was the healing of the two nations he represented. Yonamine just wanted to play ball and was never political, yet his quest led two nations once at war just a little closer together.

And in the world of Asian-American heroes, few achieved what Wally Yonamine did on and off the field.

DID YOU KNOW?

- Yonamine was married to his wife Jane until he died on February 28, 2011. The couple had two daughters, Wallis and Amy.

- Yonamine was a lefty who stood 5'9, which wasn't particularly short for baseball players in the 1950s.

- After playing for the Giants for ten years, Yonamine spent his last two years playing for the Chunichi Dragons. He retired as a player after the 1962 season.

- As Yonamine "opened" the Nippon Professional Baseball League for non-Japanese, some think he "opened" the Majors for Japanese players. In 1964, relief pitcher Mansanori Murakami was the first Japanese player to play in a Major League game, but it wouldn't be until the late 1990s that a wave of Japanese players made it to the Majors. One of the most notable players in that wave was Ichiro Suzuki who, like Yonamine, played outfield and was known for his aggressive base running.

- After retiring from managing in 1977, Yonamine and his wife opened a pearl store in Tokyo. Their two daughters ran an office of the company on Rodeo Drive in Los Angeles, California.

CHAPTER 5

Bruce Lee: Making Martial Arts Cool

Before Jean-Claude Van Damme kicked his way to stardom in the 1980s and '90s, Chuck Norris punched his way across movie screens in the 1970s and '80s. Today, many see Norris as the father of modern martial arts movies - at least in the West - and the first true badass to combine Eastern martial arts with Western fighting styles to create an entertaining illusion of an almost invincible man.

But before anyone knew who Chuck Norris was, Bruce Lee was the world's first true martial arts action hero. In fact, Lee even kicked Norris' butt (at least on the silver screen).

For a few brief years, American-born Hong Kong actor and martial artist Lee amazed audiences with his ability to perform physical feats that seemed impossible. Well, for most of us they are impossible, but for Lee challenging the impossible is just what he did.

Although born into a respected, stable family, young Lee ran the streets of Hong Kong, getting into trouble that often ended with him getting into physical fights. After coming under the influence of both White and Chinese mentors, Lee eventually channeled his anger into physical exercise and martial arts training, learning several different fighting styles along the way.

Lee then called his new form of "mixed martial arts" Jeet Kune Do, which he would teach to those of any ethnic background, as long as they had the discipline to handle the training.

As Lee's reputation as a martial arts teacher and practitioner grew, Hollywood called in 1966. Lee began acting in television and film, where he was able to showcase his abilities to a much larger audience. But before Lee's fame had come close to peaking, he died under still -mysterious circumstances.

Some think Bruce Lee died from a curse, while others think he simply overtrained.

The reality is that Bruce Lee will forever be remembered as one of the top Asian-American heroes for what he achieved in the sports *and* entertainment industries. Lee proved that Asian males could be action stars, and he played a crucial role in making martial arts films popular in the United States.

Maybe even more important, though, was Lee's legacy in combat sports. Before Lee, martial arts styles rarely mixed and the term "mixed martial arts" was unheard of. But because of Jeet Kune Do's influence, mixed martial arts (MMA) are seen today as a combat fighting style around the world.

EAST MEETS WEST

Bruce Lee was a man whose mind, body, and soul were always partially in the Eastern world and partially in the West. He was born Lee Jun-Fan (Anglicized as "Bruce") in 1940 to a father who was a Hong Kong actor and opera singer and a mother who came from a wealthy Hong Kong family. Lee's mother was of partial European heritage, though, which tied him to the West but also proved to be a wedge between him and some of the more traditional Chinese people, especially when it came to martial arts.

When Bruce was just a child his parents moved back to Hong Kong, leaving his two older sisters and an older brother in the United States. Lee maintained contact with his siblings off and on throughout his short life despite often being separated by thousands of miles.

For young Bruce, growing up in British Hong Kong had its ups and downs but was definitely interesting. Bruce began his entertainment career as a child actor in Hong Kong, but martial arts was what really interested him.

Lee constantly got into fights with other boys on the streets of Hong Kong, sometimes due to his mixed heritage, so to hone his fighting skills, he learned as many styles as he could.

While at a Catholic school in Hong Kong, Lee learned boxing from a priest and he later trained in the Wing Chun style of Kung Fu.

But learning Wing Chun wasn't easy for Lee.

For centuries, some of the Asian martial arts styles were closely guarded cultural secrets, which outsiders were forbidden from learning - and teaching outsiders was even more taboo. When the American military came to Japan and Korea in the mid-20th century, the locals taught Americans styles such as Karate and Taekwondo, which then spread throughout the US and the world.

But the Chinese styles were as closed to outsiders as most of their society was.

By the 1950s, mainland China was under communist rule and closed to most of the world, while Hong Kong was a place where secret societies known as Triads ruled the streets.

Owing to Lee's persistence and genuine interest in the style, Wing Chun master Yip Man eventually relented and taught Bruce Lee the closely held secret of Wing Chun.

Lee then combined Wing Chun with his boxing experience and numerous other fighting styles he'd learned along the way to create a style of his own called Jeet Kune Do.

Jeet Kune Do was based on realistic street fighting techniques Lee used on the streets of Hong Kong that stressed the ability to adapt to the situation. As Lee stated in his own words:

"There is no mystery about my style. My movements are simple, direct and non-classical. The extraordinary part of it lies in its simplicity. Every movement in Jeet Kune Do is being so of itself. There is nothing artificial about it. I always believe that the easy way

is the right way. Jeet Kune Do is simply the direct expression of one's feelings with the minimum of movements and energy."

Lee described the movements in Jeet Kune Do as being like an overflowing cup of water, "casting off what was useless."

So, when Lee's parents sent him to live with his older sister Agnes in San Francisco in 1959, he was ready to bring his new style to America.

RISE TO FAME

Lee spent some time in San Francisco before moving north to Seattle, which he made one of his many homes throughout the world. He married a local woman and had two children as he continued to develop and teach his unique style to Americans. He also traveled quite a bit doing demonstrations of how effective his style could be for anyone of any size.

Lee's big debut on the martial arts scene was at the 1964 Long Beach International Karate Championships in Long Beach, California. Contrary to what many people think, Lee didn't compete in official martial arts tournaments or matches. He did fight a number of street fights and unsanctioned matches, but his involvement in officially sanctioned martial arts competitions consisted of him demonstrating his amazing physical prowess.

At 5'8 and 141 pounds, Lee has a very "shredded" lean yet muscular physique. In addition to the time that he spent perfecting his unique style, he also spent a lot of time doing strength and cardiovascular training.

All of this was on display in Long Beach in 1964.

Lee wowed the crowd by doing his now-famous "two-finger pushups" using only his index fingers and thumbs, but it was his "one-inch punch" that stole the show.

As the name indicates, the one-inch punch is a punch that is thrown from less than an inch away from the target. In Lee's demonstration, he knocked a man to the floor with the one-inch punch, showing that if done properly a close contact punch can be deadly.

By the mid-1960s, Lee and his new fighting style had attracted a lot of attention, although some of it wasn't wanted.

According to legend, while Lee was living in Oakland, California in 1964, members of the Chinese secret societies ordered Lee to quit teaching Kung Fu to non-Chinese people. When Lee refused to do so, the societies sent Wong Jack-Man to challenge Lee to a fight.

If Lee lost, he had to leave town, but if he won then he could keep teaching the non-Chinese.

The winner of the match will probably never be known because both men and their supporters later claimed victory. With that said, Lee did keep teaching non-Chinese students.

But by that time Hollywood heard of Lee.

In 1966, Lee was cast as Kato, the Green Hornet's martial arts expert driver, in the superhero television show *The Green Hornet*. Although the show was only on for one season, it raised Lee's profile. *The Green Hornet* was truly a first in many ways, as it was one of the first shows on American television to highlight martial arts and it was one of the earliest depictions of an Asian male in a "tough guy" role.

But *The Green Hornet* was only the beginning of what should have been a long and fruitful career.

Lee went on to guest star in several TV shows by the early '70s was acting in Hong Kong and Hollywood films. His most notable films were *Fist of Fury* (1972), *Way of the Dragon* (1972) (where he beat up Chuck Norris), and *Enter the Dragon* (1973).

And while he was making it big in film and TV, Lee was perfecting Jeet Kune Do and teaching it to some of the biggest celebrities of the era including Steve McQueen, James Coburn, and Kareem Abdul Jabbar.

Bruce Lee had the world in the palm of his hand when tragedy struck in 1973.

THE CURSE OF BRUCE LEE?

After he finished filming *Enter the Dragon,* Lee spent most of his time in his Hong Kong home. While spending time with friends in Hong Kong on July 20, 1973, Lee began having headaches, so his friend Betty Ting give him a pill that contained aspirin and a tranquilizer. Within hours Lee was dead from a swollen brain, which doctors attributed at least partially to the pill, calling it "death by misadventure."

The amazing life of the budding action star ended prematurely at the age of 32.

Because Lee's death was so mysterious, it immediately led to speculation and even conspiracy theories. Some said Lee died from using cortisone, while others thought his death was the result of heatstroke from overwork.

Still, others believe the explanation is not of this world.

The theory that Bruce Lee's death was the result of an ancient curse may sound like something out of a horror movie at first, but it becomes frighteningly more realistic when you consider the fact that his son Brandon died in a freak accident with a prop gun in 1993.

There are generally three versions of the Lee family curse that have circulated throughout the decades since Bruce's death. The first is that Bruce's father upset some influential people in Hong Kong who then brought down a generational curse on the family. Another is that after he died, Bruce's father was buried next to a child, which is a taboo in Chinese culture that can adversely affect multiple generations of a family.

The third and most interesting of the theories is that the curse originated in San Francisco's Chinatown when Lee refused to stop teaching non-Chinese students Chinese-based martial arts. According to this theory, Lee actually lost that fight to Wong Jack-Man, and that when he didn't quit teaching his style, he was cursed.

Although most people today, Chinese and non-Chinese, don't believe Bruce Lee was the victim of a curse, all agree that he left this world much too soon. In the span of his short but influential life, Bruce Lee became a martial arts icon and an example to young Asian-American boys that they could be as tough as any of the other kids.

DID YOU KNOW?

- Bruce married his wife Linda in 1964. They had two children, Brandon, born in 1965, and Shannon, born in 1969.

- Lee died six days before *Enter the Dragon*—which is considered to be his best film—was released. Ironically, and eerily, Bruce's son Brandon died before his best film, *The Crow*, was released.

- Lee was buried in the Lake View Cemetery in Seattle, Washington. Brandon Lee was later buried next to his father, with the graves becoming tourist attractions.

- Despite being Chinese and considered a role model by Chinese people all over the world, Bruce Lee's films were banned in China for many years.

- Lee followed a strict diet that eschewed most processed foods, refined sugars, and bread.

CHAPTER 6

Christine Ha: A Recipe for Success Despite Adversity

Heroes and heroines of any background usually have to go through some pretty significant challenges in their lives before realizing their full potential and becoming important people. In this book, we've already seen how wars, bias, and tragic events, have put up barriers in front of our heroes and heroines, but each time they were able to overcome and usually get even stronger.

Yes, true heroes and heroines are unique because they *can* overcome obstacles, no matter if they are social, political, or even physical.

In the case of Vietnamese-American chef Christine Ha, she had to overcome blindness in her adulthood caused by a rare disease.

Most people can't imagine what it would be like to rapidly lose your sight as a teenager. Once the initial shock of your new reality wears off, you'd have to pretty much relearn how to do even the most mundane tasks in life.

Many people would just give up while others would struggle to accept that life would never be what they expected.

But for Christine Ma, it proved to be a challenge for her to overcome.

After Ma was diagnosed with the rare condition neuromyelitis optica, which quickly reduced her sight from 20/20 to just being able to see objects as blurs, she devoted all her time to perfecting her passion for cooking. Ha began working as a chef, which eventually led her to apply to be a contestant on the hit show *MasterChef* with the notorious, obstreperous celebrity chef, Gordon Ramsay.

Defying the odds, Ma won the third season of the show in 2012 and never looked back.

SEEING THINGS DIFFERENTLY

Life began easy enough for Christine Ha, if not a bit more interesting than the average American. She was born in Los Angeles, California in 1979 to Vietnamese refugees who needed to leave their country when the communist forces took control in 1975.

The Ha family eventually relocated to Houston, Texas, where Christine was given considerable attention as an only child, although she was never spoiled. Her parents were truly a positive force in Christine's early life, which made her mother's death all that much tougher to deal with.

Christine was only 14 when her mother died of lung cancer. Losing a parent at such an age is probably the toughest time since it is a formative period in your life. You are going through puberty and becoming more self-aware at that age, so a tragedy of such a scale can sometimes push a kid into hanging with the "wrong crowd," experimenting with drugs and/or alcohol, or even getting involved in criminal activity.

But Christine used the experience to reflect on her life, get closer with her family, and move toward her goals.

After entering college and studying finance and creative writing, Christine was faced with her next big obstacle in life - blindness.

When Ha was diagnosed with neuromyelitis optica in 2004, the prognosis was not good. It's a rare disease where the optic nerves and the spinal cord become inflamed, resulting in varying levels of blindness. For many afflicted with the disease, the symptoms are temporary and treatable with different drugs, but for Ma, it proved to be much more serious and permanent.

By 2007, she could only make out blurry images.

Of all the senses, most people consider vision to be the most important. We use our sight constantly, often unconsciously, which meant that Ma had a lot of adjustments to make, especially since she was embarking on a career as a chef!

Although you think of cooking as involving primarily taste and smell, you still need to see the portions, right? You also need to actually see what you're cooking, right?

To overcome the challenge, Ha learned to rely more on her other senses.

"I use a lot of my sense of touch, smell, taste and sound," Ha says. "My sense of taste has become more nuanced because I have one less sense to depend on."

Ha also took the disability in stride, adopting the nickname "The Blind Cook" as part of her personal branding mission.

And by 2012, all of her hard work and persistence finally paid off when she won season three of *MasterChef*.

Ha parlayed her win on *MasterChef* into hosting roles for cooking shows on Canadian and Vietnamese television as well as becoming a best-selling author, detailing her life and struggles and her unique blend of Asian-American fusion dishes.

Perhaps what has endeared Christine Ha to so many people around the world is her easygoing attitude and pleasant nature that seems so natural. Many people would've reacted with bitterness over her circumstances, but for Christine Ha, it was just another bump in the long road of life. And for that, many people with a culinary background see Christine Ha as not only a top American chef but as a genuine Asian-American heroine.

DID YOU KNOW?

- Ha opened her own restaurant in 2018 in Houston, Texas called "The Blind Goat." The word "blind" refers to her disability, while the goat is her Vietnamese zodiac sign. The food is a mix of southeast Asian with some southern US and Tex-Mex thrown in for good measure.

- Ha earned an MIS from the University of Texas, Austin, and an MA from the University of Houston.

- In addition to her television appearances, Ha has authored several articles, two books, and given a TED talk about her life.

- Ha said she develops the unique recipes for her restaurant from her many travels around the world, so in addition to a heavy Asian-American influence, you'll find European and Latin American tastes on the menu as well. "Food has become more important to me. Traveling to me is not about sightseeing, obviously," Ha says. "In order to learn about another culture, I really need to eat their food, find out what the locals eat and eat the same thing. That's how I sightsee," she said.

- Although Ha says that her mother was a great cook, she never took the time to learn from her before she died. Ha didn't start cooking until she started college and unlike many world-renowned chefs, she never went to cooking school.

CHAPTER 7

Chinese Railroad Workers: Connecting America

Today, there are more than 20 million Americans of Asian ancestry from more than 20 different countries, but the largest and most established of those are Chinese Americans. Chinese people first began arriving in the western United States in large numbers during the mid-1800s and quickly established themselves in many cities and towns along the West Coast.

By the late 1800s, Chinatown neighborhoods could be found in most major West Coast cities, and they became gathering points not just for the Chinese but for later waves of immigrants from all over the Asian continent.

The establishment of the Chinese American community wasn't easy, though.

Like their American counterparts, the first Chinese immigrants in the West had to battle against the elements, occasional Indian attacks, and more frequently the hazards of dangerous work. But unlike the Americans, the Chinese had to deal with strict Chinese emigration policies that limited how many of them could leave the country, American immigration policies that eventually excluded the Chinese from entering the US, and anti-Chinese attitudes from American workers.

Still, even with all those barriers, the first Chinese immigrants in America made significant contributions to the development of the nation's infrastructure.

After the discovery of gold in California brought tens of thousands of settlers to the new territory, it eventually became a state that was essentially an island separated from the rest of the country by what seemed to be an endless stretch of mountains, deserts, and plains. Wagon trains weren't going to efficiently connect the East to California and ships had to go all the way around the southern tip of South America.

So, the government and the railroad barons embarked on a great quest to connect the country via a transcontinental railroad.

When the "golden spike" was laid in Promontory, Utah on May 10, 1869, that connected the Central Pacific Railroad and the Union Pacific Railroad, more than 10,000 Chinese workers were among those who contributed to the achievement.

Today, most of these men aren't known by name, but there is no doubt that they were all very important.

GOLD AND CHINA

In 1849, China was an exotic country that few Americans knew about. It was halfway around the world, but it may have been on another world as far as most Americans were concerned. Although there were no real restrictions on Chinese immigration to the United States at that point—there were few immigration restrictions in general at that point in history—there was no real reason for the Chinese to brave the long voyage.

The Americans hadn't invited the Chinese and the Chinese government at the time generally prohibited its people from leaving.

The ruling Qing Dynasty of China passed decrees in the 1700s that essentially made China a closed society - outsiders were only allowed into certain places and Chinese weren't allowed to leave.

But rules are meant to be broken, right?

By the 1800s, the Qing rulers exerted little control outside of Beijing and a few other major cities, so adventurous Chinese men were beginning to take their chances more and more to work in Singapore, Malaysia, and even the United States.

The Chinese were particularly drawn to the US after hearing about the stories of gold in California.

By 1851, more than 25,000 Chinese men joined tens of thousands of European immigrants and Americans in the new state of California panning and mining for gold.

Needless to say, things weren't always easy for the Chinese miners.

They obviously looked different physically from the vast majority of the other miners in California, but they also dressed and spoke differently. Few Chinese people knew English at the time and most wore their traditional clothing.

Since most of the men left their wives and families behind in China during the first few years, they sometimes made trips back to China to either check on their families or if they made permanent homes, to bring them to America. In these cases, the men had to keep their very distinct *queue* hairstyle, which was the front half of the head shaved bald and the back half uncut and tied in a braid.

The Qing rulers required that all Chinese men wear the 19th-century mullet or face execution!

Well, the exotic look of the Chinese miners made them the object of scorn and the fact that they were competition meant that they were subject to assault, robbery, or even murder. In the ethnic hierarchy of the 19th-century American West, Chinese people were above the American Indians but were actually usually below Black and Hispanic people.

So, to mitigate the language barriers and hostilities from other miners, the Chinese formed Chinatowns that catered to the needs of Chinese workers and they tended to work more communally for protection.

As the initial gold and silver rushes wound down by the late 1850s, thousands of Chinese ex-miners were in the West to stay. Some had become successful Chinatown businessmen, a few had struck it rich in the gold and silver mines, while most were left looking for employment.

They didn't have to wait long, though.

THE GOLDEN SPIKE

In 1863, the Union Pacific and Central Pacific railroads combined their resources to complete the first transcontinental railroad in North America. The ambitious plan called for the Central to work west from Omaha and meet the Pacific, which began in Sacramento, in Utah. It would cost plenty of money, take a lot of time, and consist of plenty of workers.

At first, it wasn't clear where the railroads would find the workers. It was tough and dangerous work and at only about $1 a day, the railroads weren't paying much, even for that time. A fair number of Irish immigrants signed on, as did a spattering of Germans, Russians, Irish, and Americans, but it wasn't enough to complete the endeavor as the railroad barons wanted.

So, they looked to the Chinese immigrants.

Some railroad barons thought that since the Chinese people had proved to be good miners, they could also be good railroad workers. But others thought they were too small and weak for the job.

The Chinese workers proved to be more than fit for the task.

Chinese men ended up comprising 90% of the railroad workforce, for a total of about 10,000 workers. The railroad owners initially hired them to save money by paying them far less than American or European workers, but when they saw they were also good workers, they began importing them.

The Chinese population in America continued to grow in size due to immigration related to building the transcontinental railroad, but it also grew in influence. Chinese workers went on strike for better conditions and Chinese-American culture slowly began to take on a life of its own.

During the 1800s, more than 300,000 Chinese people came to America before the Chinese Exclusion Act ended most emigration from that country in 1882.

Possibly more than 1,000 Chinese railroad workers died completing the transcontinental railroad, which was a true sacrifice to the future of America. Although the contributions of the Chinese railroad workers were once overlooked, in more recent years researchers have noted that these men were true heroes.

DID YOU KNOW?

- Nineteenth-century Chinese immigrants in the American West have been portrayed in a number of different American television "Westerns", including the 1960s show *Bonanza*, *Kung Fu* in the 1970s, and *Deadwood* in the 2000s. For the most part, these shows depicted the Chinese immigrants in a generally sympathetic, although sometimes stereotypical light.

- After the California gold rush faded in the late 1850s, many of the Chinese miners turned to agriculture or to work as domestic servants in the cities. Others became launderers, which in 1870 was the fourth-most popular profession among Chinese immigrants in America.

- The Chinese miners were quite mobile. After the California gold rush, many moved to Colorado for the gold rush that began there in 1858. When the Comstock Lode was discovered in Nevada in 1859, sparking a silver rush, many traveled there, and when gold was discovered in the Black Hills of South Dakota in 1874, Chinese miners soon followed.

- Most of the early Chinese-American immigrants were from the Guangdong province of China. Guangdong is in southern China and is a Cantonese-speaking province.

- To protect themselves from violence from the outside, and to keep order within their communities, early Chinese

Americans formed societies known as "Tongs." The Tongs were originally benevolent, paternal societies, but in more recent decades, they have been accused of being involved in organized crime and more like a Chinese mafia than a cultural association.

CHAPTER 8

Dalip Saund:
A Congressional First

The geographical and cultural status of Indians has been a point of debate and a subject in itself for decades in many countries. It's true that India is in Asia, and therefore the people are considered Asians, but Indians clearly look different from East and Southeast Asians and are also culturally different. Hindi, the *lingua franca* of India, is related to European languages and is not connected to East Asian languages, and India has a unique history that has probably influenced East Asia more than East Asia has influenced it. After all, Buddhism, which most people associate with East Asia, originated in India.

In the United Kingdom, Indians and Pakistanis, as well as most Arabs for that matter, are referenced to as "Asians," while in the United States and Canada, Indians are considered Asian by the government, but the average person generally thinks of "Asians" as being East or Southeast Asian.

With all of that said, Indians have encountered many of the same trials as East Asians when they arrived in the United States and have produced their share of heroes as well.

Like their Chinese counterparts, many of the first Indian immigrants entered the United States on the West Coast in the 1800s, but unlike the Chinese immigrants, many came from Canada where they sought to escape anti-Indian violence and discrimination. Also, unlike the early Chinese immigrants, the Indians usually moved with their families.

Many of these early Indian immigrants worked in the timber industry of the Northwest and some worked alongside the Chinese on the railroads. Nearly all of the first wave of Indian immigrants were of the Sikh religion.

Dalip Singh Saund was one such Sikh immigrant.

Saund came to the United States as a graduate student but decided to stay and become a citizen when Indians were allowed to naturalize after World War II. Throughout his life, Saund was a tireless advocate for his people, eventually becoming the first Asian-American to be elected to the United States Congress.

Saund became a symbol for a new generation of Indian-Americans who were born in the United States, making him a true trailblazing hero in politics.

INSPIRED BY AMERICA

Dalip Singh Saund was born in 1899 to a financially successful family in the Punjab region of India. From an early age, Saund's primary interests were education and Indian liberation. Saund's parents paid for his education, which he reciprocated by achieving good marks. The young Saund had a particular aptitude for science and mathematics, but when he wasn't solving equations or formulas, he was reading up on history and political science.

Like many young Indians of the time, Saund took a particular interest in the Indian independence movement. The vast country was still part of the British Empire, and when the British reneged on their promise to give independence to India after World War I, it sparked a mass liberation movement.

Saund never really took part in any of the activism, but he did follow the lectures and speeches of Mohandas Gandhi. He also read up on Thomas Jefferson, Abraham Lincoln, and other early American leaders for inspiration.

After earning a BA in Mathematics at the University of Punjab, Saund decided that he wanted to go to America to experience the nation first hand.

But doing so would be no easy task.

American immigration laws at the time were very restrictive and favored Europeans. Saund's only chance to live in America was to get a student visa, which he acquired when the University of California, Berkley accepted him into their agricultural program.

Next, he had to convince his parents to allow him to leave.

Saund's family was considered progressive by the standards of the era, but still traditional when it came to big decisions, so he was expected to ask for permission to leave the country.

"I assured my family," he wrote in his 1960 book *Congressman From India*, "that I would study in the United States for at least two and not more than three years and would then return home."

But plans changed, with Saund not only shifting his focus to mathematics but also deciding to stay in the United States after he earned his MA in 1922 and his Ph.D. in 1924.

Still, there wasn't much an Indian, even a well-educated Indian, could do in the US in 1925. Saund could have returned to India and taught or done research, but he instead chose to move to Southern California and work alongside thousands of other Indians in the fields of the Imperial Valley.

Just like most immigrants of the era, Saund scrimped and saved until he earned enough to farm his own land, although he knew that farming would never be his lifelong vocation. In 1930, he wrote his first book, *My Mother India*, which was about the Indian independence movement. Saund was at the time an ardent Indian nationalist, but he was also becoming more ingrained into American culture.

He began spending much of his time in Los Angeles area libraries and gave lectures and speeches around Southern California about Indian nationalism, culture, and the place of Indians in American society. It was at one of these lectures where he met his future wife, Marian Kosa.

Kosa was a Czechoslovakian immigrant, and although of a different nationality and religion to Saund, she shared with him a similar immigrant story. The couple married in 1928 and later had three children.

TAKING OFFICE

Dalip Saund had big political aspirations. His dreams began with Indian independence but by the 1940s, he was focused on politics in the US. By that time, he had been living in the US for more than 20 years and considered himself to be American.

But the government at the time didn't concur.

So Saund helped organize efforts to change the naturalization laws as they pertained to Indians, and in 1946, the Luce-Cellar Act passed allowing 100 Indians to naturalize.

Saund quickly joined the waiting list and in 1949 he officially became one of the first Indian- Americans.

Then Saund moved on to his next goal: gaining political office.

Many thought Saund was joking when he announced his plans to run for the office of Justice of the Peace in Westmoreland township, California in 1950, but they were more than surprised when he won. The result was overturned, though, when it was revealed that Saund had been a citizen for less than one year, which made him ineligible.

Undeterred, Saund ran for the post again and won.

Saund was able to win the election, and later elections, by building alliances with white farmers and getting the votes of a majority of non-whites who were eligible to vote. Once he became the Justice of the Peace, he governed as a conservative by going after the town's red-light district and by working with Border Patrol to clamp down on sex workers illegally crossing the Mexican-American border.

In 1956, "Judge Saund" as he was known in the Imperial Valley, decided to try his hand at the big time by running for an open US House seat.

Saund's challenger in the Democratic primary questioned his loyalty and Americanness, but by that time the Judge had built enough of a coalition to push through that issue. The real question would be if he could defeat his Republican challenger, Jacqueline Odlum.

It was the era of Eisenhower and the California electorate was much whiter and more conservative than it is currently, yet Saund still beat Odlum by more than 3,000 votes.

Dalip Saund served three terms in Congress before a severe stroke left him debilitated and unable to campaign in the 1962 election. Although Saund left public life after losing the 1962 election, he left a lasting and important legacy on the American cultural and political landscapes. He opened the door for others of Indian and Asian ancestry to run for political office and showed that sometimes one person really can change things.

DID YOU KNOW?

- Saund's tuition was paid for by the Stockton, California Gurdwara. A gurdwara is essentially a Sikh temple or church, and the Stockton Gurdwara is the oldest and first gurdwara in the United States.

- While in graduate school, Saund spent his summers working in canneries and even made his way into management with a company.

- The name "Singh" means lion in a number of Indo-European languages in South Asia, including Punjabi, the language of the Sikhs. In the 1700s, the Sikh Guru Gobind Singh mandated that all male Sikhs take the name.

- Saund's political positions were fairly moderate for the period but would probably be considered conservative by today's standards. He was against racial segregation domestically, but he was also anti-communist and more or less supported Eisenhower's "domino theory," although not with the use of force.

- After farming for more than 20 years Saund started a fertilizer business in Westmorland while living with his family near Los Angeles. During that period, he commuted about 1,000 miles a week.

CHAPTER 9

Michio Kaku: Making Science Easier to Understand

As we go through our day-to-day routine of work, play, and family, most of us pay little attention to how everything works. We may briefly think about how taxes are paid and how our governments function, but very few of us spend much time contemplating how atoms interact, how cells divide, or the limits of the universe.

Some of that is fun and maybe good fodder for science-fiction movies, but most of us just don't have the time to think about it at all.

And let's face it, most of us probably don't have the patience either. When it comes to science, unless you're a scientist, most of us just don't understand what's being said. When the average scientist speaks, it may as well be in an alien language to most of us.

But since science is a part of all our lives, and understanding it is vital to create a better society, some scientists have made it their mission to make science "cool" and easier for non-specialists to understand. These scientists, who work to bring science to the masses by making it fun and easier to understand, are sometimes known as "popular scientists" and the science they promote is known as "pop-science" or "PopSci."

Bill Nye and Neil deGrasse Tyson are the two most visible popular scientists today, but before they were around, Michio Kaku wrote books, gave lectures, and appeared on television shows to promote pop-science.

Born in California to immigrant parents from Japan, Kaku was fortunate enough to avoid the internment camps and to be raised in a family that nurtured his natural curiosity and desire to learn. Kaku would earn his place in academia among the intellectual heavyweights in science and math of the 1970s, but as the young Japanese-American scholar witnessed great social changes taking place in America at the time, he knew that he could be influential beyond the ivory tower.

Michio Kaku determined that he would make complex scientific concepts and theories understandable and even fun. It definitely wasn't an easy endeavor, but most would agree that based on the popularity of his shows and the emergence of other popular scientists, Kaku's mission has been a success.

NATURAL CURIOSITY

Michio Kaku's fascinating journey through science and life began in 1947 as the world was transitioning into the post-war era. Kaku's parents were second-generation Japanese-Americans living in California, but if you remember from earlier chapters, that wasn't enough to spare them from being sent to internment camps.

Like so many young people in the camps, Kaku's parents met, fell in love, and had Michio's older brother in the camp before they were all released.

Fortunately for Michio, his parents shielded him from the pain of even knowing about the internment camps until he was a little older. For him, life was fairly easy growing up in the San Francisco Bay Area, as his parents indulged his natural scientific curiosities.

By the time he was a teen, Kaku had developed a particular affinity for physics.

He voraciously read anything on the subject of physics, became an acolyte of Einstein's theories, and began conducting experiments of his own at home.

He created a small particle accelerator in his parent's garage with the ultimate goal of creating antimatter. Although Kaku didn't create antimatter - and he did raise the ire of his mother by blacking out power in the house - the experiment was good enough to land him a spot in the National Science Fair where he earned the Hertz Engineering Scholarship to attend Harvard University.

By the late 1960s, Kaku's curiosity and hard work were starting to pay off. He graduated at the top of his physics class in 1968 and seemed destined to land a lucrative position with the government, a research lab, or at a top graduate school.

But the Vietnam War was raging and Uncle Same needed bodies. After graduating, Kaku was no longer exempt from the draft, so when his "number came up" in 1968, he was obligated to report for service.

Due to his education, Kaku thought he'd probably be assigned to a technical unit, although he soon found out that he would be just another grunt in the infantry.

As he trained to fight and possibly become one of the 500 Americans who were dying in Vietnam in the late '60s, a bit of biology came to the future popular scientist's aid.

"Then, by '69, '70, the war was beginning to wind down, and then my doctor found that I had too much sugar in my blood - I said, why didn't you find that before? So, I wrote a letter to my draft board saying that I'm 'not fit' to be part of the infantry because there's too much sugar in my blood, I'm borderline, not really diabetic," Kaku remembered in a 2014 interview. "All of a sudden, it was as if a voice up there said, 'I'm going to give you back your life. You were destined to die on some unnamed hill in Vietnam; unsung, just buried in mud, forgotten by everybody. That was your destiny.' But something happened; somebody up there changed their mind."

Call it fate, destiny, or God - Kaku certainly wouldn't call it God - it may have saved his life. However, or whatever was behind the turn of events, Kaku made the most of it. He entered graduate school at the University of California, Berkley, earning a Ph.D. in physics in 1972.

Kaku went on to lecture, teach, conduct research, and publish his work in academic journals and books throughout the 1970s. Kaku was at the vanguard of string theory and quantum physics, yet something was missing.

He believed science was the most important subject kids should learn, but it was usually at the bottom of any list. Kaku reasoned that a big part of the problem was its accessibility.

MAKING SCIENCE FUN

For guys like Michio Kaku, science and math come easy, but for most people, even most intelligent people, difficult scientific concepts can be hard to grasp. As Kaku did serious academic research and writing on physics in the 1970s and into the '80s, he began to see this inaccessibility as a problem. He reasoned that if the world in general, and the United States in particular, were to move forward, then young people would have to embrace science.

So, Kaku decided to embark on a crusade to make science more interesting, understandable, and fun for the average person, particularly kids.

Michio Kaku intended to make science cool.

And making science cool to Generation X and beyond was no easy task. It was much easier for Bruce Lee to make martial arts cool than it was, or has been, for Kaku to make science cool, or even accessible.

But if one person has been able to make strides in this regard it's been Kaku.

Kaku began writing popular science books, such as *Beyond Einstein: The Cosmic Quest for the Theory of the Universe* (1987), *Visions: How Science Will Revolutionize the 21st Century* (1997), and his most recent publication *The God Equation: The Quest for a Theory of Everything* (2021).

He has also made numerous appearances on television, radio, and podcast talk shows, hosted specials on educational TV programs and given numerous lectures at a variety of different venues. Kaku's writing, as well as his spoken presentations, are full of plenty of quips and anecdotal humor, delivered in a down-to-earth style that is easy to follow and understand.

Kaku's work has made him wealthy, and a cultural icon who's easily recognizable with his now grey long hair. It's no doubt been a good and fun ride for Kaku, but he's adamant about what his goals are. In a 2014 interview, Kaku explained in detail how his mission is to ultimately raise scientific knowledge among American kids.

"I'll go where people invite me because I want to try to excite young people to go into science. Science is the engine of prosperity, and we can't create enough scientists, I think. To keep America prosperous and healthy and alive, we have to have more scientists and we have to have more engagement of young people. For example, we have one of the worst science educational systems in science known to science. It's awful," Kaku said. "Our high school kids scored dead last among the other industrialized nations. Our students scored a little bit above the students of Jordan in many math and science exams. That's not sustainable. You cannot sustain a scientific establishment when we have one of the worst educational systems known to science, in high school. College, of course, makes up for it. Our colleges are not bad - they're top rank - but our high schools are abysmally bad."

Thanks to Kaku, many in the younger generation do see science as being exciting and fun, which brings a little bit more hope to the future!

DID YOU KNOW?

- Kaku's parents and older brother were interned at the Tule Lake War Relocation Center in California during the war, which also happened to be one of the camps where Pat Morita and his family were interned.

- Kaku has generally stayed out of politics, although he participated in the anti-nuclear movement of the 1980s and has been an advocate of stopping climate change.

- Beginning in the 1990s, Kaku began writing about Futurology, making some predictions that ultimately have come true. He wrote that in 2020 we'd be able to get on the internet with our eyeglasses and that personalized gene sequencing would be a reality.

- Despite being a world-renowned scholar, Kaku is a bit indifferent toward academic accolades, saying, "I began to realize that if I'm just Joe Blow in the street saying that I want social change, who's going to listen to you? If you have a Ph.D., if you're a professor, more people will listen to you. And so, then I realized that even though at one point, I thought a Ph.D. is kind of useless, society does treasure professors and their thoughts so why don't I become a professor and determine my own destiny."

- Kaku had two daughters, Alyson and Michelle, with his wife Shizue.

CHAPTER 10

Queen Liliuokalani: Heroine to Her People

You probably know that Texas was for a time an independent nation, but did you know the same was true for Hawaii? Before Hawaii was a state, it was a territory, but long before it was a territory, it was the Hawaiian Kingdom.

The Hawaiian Kingdom began when Kamehameha I conquered the Hawaiian Islands, putting them under the rule of the dynasty he established in 1795. The Hawaiians, who were (and still are) of Polynesian ancestry, were a fiercely independent people but by the 1800s, they were caught in the middle of the colonial rush. The British controlled most of the world, but the Americans were continually moving west under the philosophy of the Manifest Destiny, and once the North American frontier was conquered, many began looking out into the Pacific.

Eventually, American military adventurists, industrialists, and expansionists set their eyes on the Hawaiian Islands.

By the late 1800s, Hawaii had suffered a series of pandemics and was constantly being pressured by American interests. The culmination of these conflicts took place in 1887 when wealthy Americans and Hawaiians conspired to force the king to sign a new constitution at bayonet point, which earned the document the title "The Bayonet Constitution."

Those behind the coup argued that it benefited Hawaiians by disenfranchising the Asian landowners, but the truth was it kept the elites in power and gave them more land. With the royalty relegated to figureheads, the American and Hawaiian elites thought they could do as they wished.

They didn't consider Queen Liliuokalani.

Liliuokalani ascended the Hawaiian throne in 1891. Most of the oligarchs thought she'd be a nice, pliant ruler (she was married to an American, after all), but she stunned everyone by drafting a new constitution that restored the power of the monarchy and re-enfranchised many of those who lost their lands and rights under the Bayonet Constitution.

Although Liliuokalani was ultimately unsuccessful, she became a heroine of the Hawaiian people and as a symbol of resistance to 19th-century colonialism.

PRIVILEGE IN PARADISE

Today, the state of Hawaii is often referred to as "a paradise" because of its natural beauty, climate, and relatively isolated location. As mentioned earlier, though, Hawaii had endured a series of foreign invasions and internal discord in the 1800s, making it a very unstable place at times.

When the future Queen Liliuokalani was born as Lydia Lili'u Loloku Walania Kamaka'eha in 1838 on the island of Oahu, great changes were taking place all around her. The French briefly conquered the islands in 1849, which was followed by a gradual increase in American and European influence.

But for Liliuokalani, none of those things mattered much. She came from Hawaiian royalty and was educated in schools with other kids from her class.

Liliuokalani's teachers were Protestant missionaries, which is how she was introduced to the Christian faith that she devoutly followed for the rest of her life. Liliuokalani took an ecumenical approach to religion, helping to unite all Hawaiians who professed Christian beliefs, and it was her deep belief in faith that helped her through the difficult situations that she later faced.

While a schoolgirl, Liliuokalani also developed an interest in music and discovered she had an aptitude for it. The young princess picked up the native Hawaiian instrument the ukulele like a fish to water and soon after she learned several other instruments and musical styles.

Throughout her life, Liliuokalani composed many original compositions and preserved many of Hawaii's traditional songs and dances. Today, Liliuokalani's songs are played widely across Hawaii, including "Aloha Oe."

Liliuokalani also enjoyed writing essays and even wrote a book about the history of Hawaii titled *Hawai'i's Story by Hawai'i's Queen*.

As Liliuokalani wrote songs and poetry, she was given a fair amount of freedom within the royal house, even being allowed to choose her own husband, American John Owen Dominis.

Dominis was born in Hawaii to American parents and made his living as a sea merchant. He eventually worked his way into the graces of the Hawaiian royal family, who were looking to add American and European advisors to keep up with the rapidly modernizing world. He married Liliuokalani in 1862 and as a result, became the Royal Governor of Oahu.

Although the marriage was not a happy one, as Dominis was a serial philanderer, Liliuokalani came into her own as a woman and a monarch while she was married. Liliuokalani served as regent when her brother, King Kalakaua, went on a world tour in 1881 to alert leaders to the destruction of Hawaiian culture. It's arguable if the tour had any serious impact on the overall situation, but it did influence Liliuokalani to take similar stands later in her life.

While her brother was on the tour, Liliuokalani ruled in his stead, which gave her a taste of power and all the responsibilities that came with it.

ON HER OWN

When Liliuokalani's brother died while visiting the United States in January 1891, she became the queen regent of Hawaii. Liliuokalani could have just enjoyed her status and lived the rest of her life in comfort, but she instead decided to challenge the status quo and stand up for her people.

When Liliuokalani became queen, the Hawaiian government was a constitutional monarchy, so most of the government's power came from the elected legislature. In 1893, Queen Liliuokalani proposed a new constitution that would restore voting and property rights to the native Hawaiians and Asians who'd had theirs stripped with the Bayonet Constitution.

The idea was popular with Hawaiians of all classes and ethnicities, but it wasn't popular among Liliuokalani's most trusted advisors.

Almost two years to the day after she took power, Queen Liliuokalani was deposed in an American-led military coup on January 17, 1893.

Liliuokalani was imprisoned in 1895 after pro-monarchist Americans attempted to launch a rebellion on her behalf. She served over one year of house arrest in the royal palace before she was pardoned in 1896.

Hawaii was officially annexed by the United States and became a territory in 1898, but Liliuokalani made one last attempt to keep Hawaii under native rule. She brought a lawsuit against the federal government in 1909 that demanded Hawaiian crown lands be returned.

The former queen lost the case.

Liliuokalani lived out her life in peace and relative obscurity on her beloved islands, dying in Honolulu at the age of 79 in 1917. In recent years, as native Hawaiians in particular and Pacific Islanders, in general, have developed an interest in their culture and history, Queen Liliuokalani has become a source of pride and reverence. She fought for her people, peacefully, for her entire life, always maintaining a sense of dignity in the process.

DID YOU KNOW?

- Liliuokalani could not conceive children but adopted three Hawaiian children over her life. One of the children, John Dominis, was actually her husband's son with a mistress, conceived while they were married.

- After Liliuokalani became queen, John Owen Dominis was elevated to the position of prince consort. He died just months later.

- Liliuokalani's birth name, Lili'u Loloku Walania Kamaka'eha, refers to physical features, and following Hawaiian tradition, events that took place when she was born. The names are translated as: *lili'u* (smarting), *loloku* (tearful), *walania* (a burning pain), and *kamaka'eha* (sore eyes). "Lydia" was her Christian name that she was given after she was baptized.

- In 1887, Liliuokalani attended Queen Victoria's Royal Jubilee in London, England. She and her entourage traveled by ship from Hawaii to California and then by rail across the United States. She met with American President Grover Cleveland before continuing on a ship to the United Kingdom.

- Although Liliuokalani identified as an Episcopalian Christian, in 1901, she visited Joseph F. Smith, the Mormon president at the time and nephew of Joseph Smith, the founder of the Church of Latter-Day Saints. Mormons claim she was baptized into their church during that visit, although other sources dispute that claim.

CHAPTER 11

Andrew Yang: Challenging the System and Having Fun Doing It

If you've followed politics in America at all over the last two years, then you've probably heard of Andrew Yang, the Taiwanese American Democratic presidential candidate who had some pretty bold and interesting ideas. You probably also noticed that Yang has quite a unique personality and his approach to politics is unorthodox, to say the least.

Yang used his increased profile to speak about things that mattered to him and - he believed - to most Americans, such as job displacement through automation.

The idea that "robots" will replace the human workforce has been around for some time and has even been the subject of sci-fi books and movies such as *I, Robot*; but the reality is, no one in politics took the idea very seriously until Yang.

Running a quirky campaign that was as unique as himself, Yang drew considerable media attention and plenty of followers - who became known as the "Yang Gang" - as he warned of the labor and economic problems that the inevitable move toward automation will cause. His answer - universal basic income (UBI), or a guaranteed income, for displaced workers - was blasted by many, including those in his own party, as naïve and unrealistic, yet he won by getting people to actually talk about the concept.

Although Yang dropped out of the race and later endorsed Joe Biden for president, some of his ideas were adopted by the other candidates to a certain extent.

But long before Andrew Yang decided to become one of just a handful of Asian-Americans to have ever run for president, he was a successful businessman and philanthropist. Yang started several companies and non-profit organizations that made plenty of money for him and helped raise his public profile.

Yang has shown that he is a multi-talented individual with an amazing prescience for the course of technology. As technology continues to advance at a rapid pace, no doubt Andrew Yang will be there to help people understand their role in this ever-changing technological world.

BIG SHOES TO FILL

Some people who've done great things were born with low expectations. They were raised in an environment where they weren't expected to do much, and often had little support, but despite that, they later went on to become influential people.

This wasn't the case with Andrew Yang.

Yang was born into a very successful family in upstate New York in 1975. His parents were both Taiwanese immigrants. His father, Kei Hsiung, gained a Ph.D. in physics and did research and created inventions throughout his life. Yang's mother, Nancy, has an MA in statistics and his older brother has a Ph.D. in psychology.

So, from an early point in his life, Andrew Yang had some pretty big shoes to fill. This type of family life is usually beneficial and conducive to success, but it can also sometimes have the opposite effect, with children from high-achieving families rebelling by using drugs, alcohol, or becoming involved in criminal activity.

But Yang was no rebel, at least not when he was a kid. He spent most of his time studying and even skipped a year in high school, graduating early and going on to earn a BA at Brown University in 1996 and a law degree from Columbia University in 1999.

For Yang, the next step was to land a high-paying job at an elite East Coast law firm. He didn't have any problem finding such a job, but after just five months, he'd had enough of corporate law.

Yang didn't dwell on his change of career very long. As he's said in numerous interviews, "I'm a problem solver," so he looked at his career change as something to be solved.

Yang decided to try his hand at business, helping to launch an internet startup in 2000. The company, called Stargiving, was based on connecting wealthy celebrities with causes to fund, but as good an idea as the company may have been, it was the wrong time in history for the idea.

The dot-com bubble burst, putting an end to many such ventures, and in 2002, Stargiving also became a victim.

Undeterred, though, in 2006, Yang became the CEO of a test preparation company called Manhattan Prep. Although primarily a brick-and-mortar company that helped prospective graduate students undertake study for the GMAT exams, under Yang's leadership, Manhattan Prep expanded to 69 locations and began developing an online presence.

In 2009, Manhattan Prep was bought by test preparation giant Kaplan Inc, making CEO Yang a wealthy man.

Yang was able to leave the company and focus on creating nonprofit organizations, such as Venture for America (VFA).

VFA's mission is unique among nonprofits, as it aims to train recent college graduates to become startup leaders in major cities. Yang argues that long term, VFA will help create jobs in many struggling urban areas. Yang's goal of VFA creating

100,000 jobs by 2025 will unfortunately not be realized, as the organization has so far only created 4,000 jobs, but Yang remains optimistic.

"In order for organizations to have a very high ceiling, you need to set the goal very, very aggressively," Yang said when asked about not hitting the mark of 100,000 jobs by 2025.

Still, there's no denying that VFA has been a positive force in some cities and for many people, so in 2011 President Obama recognized Yang's achievements by making him a "Champion of Change" and in 2015 as a Presidential Ambassador for Global Entrepreneurship.

Yang's easy mix of activism and entrepreneurship was attractive to many Americans, especially young ones, so much so that in 2017, the businessman decided to throw his hat in the ring for the Democratic nominee in the 2020 presidential election.

THE YANG GANG

When Yang's presidential campaign began in 2019, most people didn't know what to think of him. Unlike most of the other candidates, he wasn't a lifelong politician. Also, unlike most of the other candidates, he didn't spend much time attacking President Trump. Instead, he focused on his ideas of UBI and overhauling the American educational system to promote science and math.

He came up with some pretty catchy slogans too, such as "Make America Think Harder" (MATH), "Humanity First," and "Not Left, Not Right, Forward."

The fact that Yang was Asian-American also set him apart from the other candidates; he is only the third Asian-American to mount a serious campaign for the presidency.

And make no mistake, it was a serious campaign.

Populism was exactly what catapulted Donald Trump into the White House in 2016, and early polls showed that Yang was drawing support from Trump supporters. Yang also appealed to younger, non-affiliated voters who loved to "meme" their support for him on internet message boards and social media.

Eventually, Yang's most ardent supporters became known as the "Yang Gang."

But the American political system is a cynical place that is often a club closed to outsiders. The Yang Gang hoped their guy would kick down the doors of the Democrat club the way Trump did for the Republicans in 2016, but it was not to be.

Although Yang consistently polled better than many other candidates, the major media outlets covered his campaign far less. After doing poorly in the New Hampshire primary, Yang dropped out of the race on February 11, 2020.

If you're in the Yang Gang, don't worry, because, in January 2021, Yang announced his candidacy for mayor of New York City in the June 2021 election. As the election approaches, it's likely the quirky candidate will have something up his sleeve that will draw attention to the election and his campaign. Even if he loses, though, I doubt we've heard the last of Andrew Yang or the Yang Gang.

DID YOU KNOW?

- In 2018, Yang's book *The War on Normal People: The Truth About America's Disappearing Jobs and Why Universal Basic Income Is Our Future* was published. The book relates Yang's core philosophies concerning automation and job displacement and how he thinks UBI will help the country transition into a new era.

- Yang married his wife Evelyn, who is also of Chinese ancestry, in 2011. The couple had two sons.

- Yang's specific program of UBI called for every American to get $1,000 a month from the government. He called this ambitious plan a "Freedom Dividend." He planned to pay for the Freedom Dividend by introducing a value-added tax on major corporations, including most of the tech companies. Needless to say, Yang's support from Silicon Valley wasn't so great.

- Although Yang became a wealthy man while at Manhattan Prep, his net worth in 2019 was *only* $1 million, which put him considerably below most of the other Democrat candidates, including the eventual winner and lifelong politician Joe Biden who is estimated to be worth $9 million.

- Yang is a practicing Christian and attends a Reformed Church in New Platz, New York with his family.

CHAPTER 12

Iwao Takamoto:
The Father of Scooby-Doo

Although the era of Saturday morning cartoons was relatively short-lived, it was an important part of American pop culture. From the late 1960s through the 1980s, American kids of all backgrounds, and from every corner of the country, woke up early every Saturday morning to tune into their favorite cartoons.

Everything from Yogi Bear to Spiderman and from Captain Caveman to the Herculoids was on throughout the era.

The cartoons of that time often took on lives of their own, leading to clothing and toy lines - some even inspired video games.

The truth is, though, that most of these cartoons were very short-lived, often not lasting more than ten episodes.

There's a good chance you don't remember *Help! . . . It's the Hairbear Bunch!* And you've probably never seen an episode of *The Roman Holidays*, but I can almost guarantee you've seen plenty of episodes of Scooby-Doo, right?

Beginning in 1969, the lovable but cowardly Great Dane 'Scooby-Doo' first came on the small screen in the Saturday morning cartoon show *Scooby-Doo, Where Are You!* The character and the show were an immediate hit, spawning several sequels and spin-offs that continue to this day.

Behind the idea of Scooby-Doo - his father, if you will - was Japanese-American artist Iwao Takamoto.

Takamoto was a skilled artist who had to battle through many of the same barriers other Japanese-Americans we've met in this book faced. As Takamoto spent time in an internment camp after the Pearl Harbor attack, he turned the otherwise awful situation to his advantage by finding and developing his talent for art.

Within a few short years of being released from the camp, Takamoto was making it big as a professional cartoonist in Hollywood.

Takamoto would eventually go on to be a major part of the Hanna-Barbara company, which was *the* cartoon company of the '70s, working as an artist and producer.

When it comes to Asian-American artists or any artist, for that matter, few have had the impact on modern pop culture that Iwao Takamoto has. After all, most people know little about Impressionism, post-Impressionism, Pop Art, and other esoteric art styles, but just about everyone knows who Scooby-Doo is!

INSPIRATION IN ADVERSITY

Born in Los Angeles, California in 1925, Takamoto's early years were relatively normal and carefree. Both his parents were Japanese immigrants who allowed young Iwao plenty of intellectual freedom to explore different subjects and to indulge his creative side. Takamoto worked hard in school and graduated high school with good marks.

But as Takamoto began looking for work in southern California, the Japanese attacked Pearl Harbor, which forever changed the course of his life, for good and bad.

Like nearly every Japanese family living on the West Coast at the time, and like Pat Morita's and Michio Kaku's families, the Takamotos were sent to live in the Manzanar internment camp for World War II.

Manzanar was located on the windswept Owens Valley on the western slope of the Sierra Nevada Mountains in central California. As depressing as the camp was due to the very nature of its existence, it was located in a hot, dry, and desolate region of California. That only seemed to add to the feeling of hopelessness that many of the camp internees experienced.

It definitely was a big adjustment for Takamoto, but he decided to make the best of the situation by expressing what he saw, felt, and did in Manzanar, through art. The problem was, though, Takamoto had no formal art training.

But if you know anything about art, especially artists, then you know that only techniques can be taught. What makes artists great are usually innate, natural abilities, which Takamoto had plenty of. He just needed some help.

Sometimes life has a strange way of working out. As bad as it was to be imprisoned in the Manzanar camp, it was there that Takamoto met two fellow detainees who happened to work in the graphic design and illustration business in Southern California. From these men, Takamoto learned proper drawing techniques, and perhaps most important, he made contacts he'd use once the war was over.

For the remainder of the war, Takamoto continued to draw scenes of life in the camp that he used for his portfolio.

When the war ended, the ebullient Takamoto sent his resume and portfolio to all the major studios and was hired by Walt Disney Animation Studios in 1945 as an "in-betweener."

It was during these early years with Walt Disney where Takamoto really learned the ins and outs of the animation business and slowly but surely began to establish himself in the business.

While at Disney, Takamoto worked with top animators such as Bob Connellson, Milt Kahl, and others helping design the characters in *Cinderella* (1950), *Peter Pan* (1953), *Lady and the Tramp* (1955), *Sleeping Beauty* (1959), and *One Hundred and One Dalmatians* (1961).

MAKING SCOOBY-DOO

By the early 1960s, technology was changing the nature of the entertainment industry, and Takamoto saw what lay ahead. The emergence of television as a primary technology and medium rapidly changed the way films were made. The expensive feature-length animated films that Takamoto worked on would always have a place in the entertainment landscape, but TV would be the primary medium where most American kids would consume animated shows from the mid-60s onward.

Takamoto knew this and so did his future boss, Joseph Barbera of the famous and influential Hanna-Barbara Productions Inc.

"I don't think it means a darn thing to kids whether we put in 40,000 drawings or 4,000, so long as the entertainment is there," said Barbara when asked about how his company would compete against the likes of Disney.

For Takamoto, the change in media, combined with his talent and ideas, meant that he was assured to be a success.

As Hanna-Barbera found early success with the *Tom and Jerry* series and the primetime show *The Flintstones*, the next logical step was to jump into the burgeoning Saturday morning cartoon market in the late 1960s.

Hanna-Barbera's first big Saturday morning cartoon hit was *Scooby-Doo, Where Are You!* CoWhich ran original shows on

CBS for two seasons and reruns until a new series of the crime-fighting dog and his teen companions were made.

The premise of Scooby-Doo was based on the early 1960s live-action television show *The Many Loves of Dobie Gillis* and the 1940s radio serial *I Love a Mystery*. The plots were silly and unrealistic, even to kids, but for most kids, it didn't matter because they all tuned in to see Takamoto's creation -Scooby-Doo

Takamoto later said that Barbera wanted the teens' dog to be a Great Dane, so he researched what a prize-winning Great Dane should look like and basically created the opposite.

"I decided to go the opposite and gave him a hump back, bowed legs, big chin and such," Takamoto noted in a later interview. "Even his color is wrong."

Takamoto also received inspiration from one of his earlier creations, the dog Astro from the early '60s animated series *The Jetsons*.

But Takamoto's laid-back, creative personality sensed what American kids would think was funny and cool at that time. And Takamoto knew what kids liked all through the 1970s and '80s.

As Takamoto worked on Scooby-Doo for other shows and created an entire family of Scooby's relatives, he began producing cartoons for Hanna-Barbera in the '70s. Takamoto was involved as either an artist or producer in just about every hit Hanna-Barbera show of the era, including: *Josie and the Pussycats, The Great Grape Ape Show, Hong Kong Phooey,* and *Jabber Jaw.*

By the time the Saturday morning cartoon era ended in the late 1980s/early 1990s, Takamoto's footprint on the animation and cartoon industry was immense. A generation of cartoonists and illustrators who grew up watching his creations during the '70s and '80s were themselves entering the industry. Although they were using technology that Takamoto didn't have at his disposal, his ideas and attitudes influenced each and every one of them.

Few American artists of any background can match Iwao Takamoto's talent or the amount of joy that he brought to millions of children from coast to coast.

DID YOU KNOW?

- Takamoto was married twice and had one child with his first wife.

- Several factors fueled Takamoto's early success, including his natural talent, amiable personality, and ambition, but his ability to adapt to new styles and techniques also played a role. Although he used traditional animation "cel art," he used individual frames as pictures in their own right to create more realistic movement and a very distinct "Hanna-Barbera style."

- Later in his life, Takamoto was recognized by his peers for his achievements and contributions to the field. He was awarded the Winsor McCray Award in 1996 for lifetime contributions in the field of animation and the Golden Award in 2005 from the Animation Guild for his achievements in the animation industry.

- Not every show Takamoto worked on was a hit. You probably don't remember the Saturday morning cartoon *Inch High, Private Eye* because only 13 episodes were made. Takamoto was the producer on the show and although the animation was up to par, the premise of an inch-high detective based on TV spy Maxwell Smart didn't go over well with kids in 1973.

- Takamoto died on January 8, 2007, at the age of 81 from a heart attack while in Los Angeles. His body was interred at the Mount Sinai Memorial Park Cemetery in Los Angeles, California.

CHAPTER 13

Har Gobind Khorana: From Poverty to the Nobel Prize

Today, the field of genetics is being developed at a lightning speed. Even if science doesn't interest you, you certainly will have at least heard about DNA, genetics, and cloning. Maybe you've even heard about gene sequencing or polymerase chain reactions? All of these ideas and processes are the result of decades of experiments, plenty of trial and error, and the work of countless scientists.

But if you go back far enough in the field of chemical biology, you'll come across the name Har Gobind Khorana.

Khorana was one of the most influential scientists in world history because his theories and experiments led to the birth of the scientific sub-discipline of chemical biology, which is where all of those above-listed discoveries and concepts come from.

Khorana rose from being an obscure scientist from India with some interesting ideas about the composition of enzymes and proteins to being a world-renowned scholar who changed the way we see the building blocks of life. His revolutionary work was eventually recognized with a Nobel Prize, but like many of the heroes and heroines in our book, Khorana's success didn't come without some serious challenges.

Khorana was born into poverty in a region of the world that can be described as a sea of illiteracy at the time. But due to a combination of natural intelligence and hard work, Khorana was able to rise above the limitations of his childhood and realize his dreams.

He also inspired a new generation of young people to enter into the scientific field despite being poor or having other obstacles that seemingly hold them back.

Perhaps most important, though, is that Khorana's important work led to scientific breakthroughs that continue to this day. Most of us probably don't understand all the details of

Khorana's work - I know I don't! - but we live with it every day, all around us.

Thanks to Har Gobind Khorana, we all know a lot more about what we're all made of!

A DESIRE TO LEARN

Har Gobind Khorana was born in 1922 in a small village called Raipur in the Punjab province of what is today Pakistan, and what was at the time British India. Since Khorana and his family were Hindus, Khorana would later come to be seen as Indian, and when he became an American citizen in 1966, Indian-American.

Khorana grew up in a poor but proud family. He was the youngest of five children in a family headed by a father who was a taxation clerk and a devout Hindu.

The people of Khorana's village were known to be hardworking, friendly, and devoutly religious, but not particularly literate. For most Indians at the time, literacy and education were things only the more affluent urban dwellers enjoyed; for those in villages such as Raipur, you learned how to do the job of your father and that was it.

Luckily for Khorana, though, literacy was a requirement of his father's job, and his father was an ardent believer in education. Khorana later reflected on his father's desire to educate him and his siblings:

"Although poor, my father was dedicated to educating his children and we were practically the only literate family in the village inhabited by about 100 people."

Khorana attended the equivalent of high school in the nearby city of Multan, where his teachers were impressed with his discipline and ability to learn the material quickly.

Due to his high marks, Khorana had no problem being accepted into a number of universities in British India, although funding was immediately a concern. University tuition, in general, was much lower in the 1940s, but when the cost of living was factored into it, Khorana was facing a pretty stiff challenge. So, he applied for and received several scholarships that paid his tuition and helped him with some living expenses.

Still, he had to pinch every penny as he studied at Punjab University in Lahore (today Pakistan), earning a BA in 1943 and an MA in 1945, in chemistry and biochemistry.

Graduating with those degrees in those fields was quite an achievement, so Khorana thought he wouldn't have a problem finding work in one of British India's major cities, but things were tough all over at that time. World War II was just winding down and the Indian independence movement was kicking into high gear, so people with advanced degrees in chemical biology weren't a high priority.

The truth is not many people really knew what chemical biology was at the time. But in less than 20 years, everyone in the science world would know what chemical biology was and they would know the name Har Gobind Khorana.

CREATING CHEMICAL BIOLOGY

Before Khorana, the fields of chemistry and biology were thought to be distinct and separate. Yes, there was overlap in some areas, but for the most part, scholars were experts in one *or* the other field.

Then Khorana changed all that by introducing the new scientific study—you could even say a new paradigm - of chemical biology.

But before he became the father of chemical biology, Khorana had to prove himself in the field. The Indian government knew that he had the tools needed to be a success, and since India was on the verge of independence in 1945 and knew it needed future leaders, it awarded Khorana and several other young Indians with impressive backgrounds scholarships to study in graduate programs around the world.

Khorana was admitted into the doctoral program at the University of Liverpool in 1945, where he earned a Ph.D. in Organic Chemistry in 1948.

The bright Indian scientist wanted to return to his native India, but things were still unstable so he moved around the world quite a bit, working at universities and labs in Switzerland, England, Canada, and the United States. It was his work at the University of Wisconsin, Madison, however, that had the biggest impact on the world.

From 1960 to 1970, Khorana worked with some of the best biologists and chemists in the world at the University of Wisconsin. The university, city, and country became his adopted home and in 1966 he became an American citizen.

But as much as Khorana appreciated all the opportunities and everything his new country did for him, he wanted to give something even bigger back to the country.

Khorana, along with his colleagues Robert Holley and Marshal Nirenberg, worked long hours at their Madison lab to work on coding ribonucleic acid (RNA) to synthesize certain proteins. Their combined work led to a 1968 Nobel Prize in physiology or medicine.

Perhaps the most important part of the breakthrough is that it led to the creation of the field of chemical biology, opening the door for everything we know about DNA today.

But Khorana kept doing important work long after he won his Nobel Prize.

In 1972, Khorana built the first artificial gene, and four years later, he was able to show that an artificial gene can function within a bacterial cell.

I'll be honest, the details of most of what Gobind Khorana did are over my head, but I'm smart enough to know that the impact he made on the world was immense, which makes him a true Indian-American hero.

DID YOU KNOW?

- After working in Wisconsin for ten years, Khorana left for the even more prestigious Massachusetts Institute of Technology (MIT) in 1970, where he worked until he retired in 2007.

- Khorana's Nobel Prize was just the first of many awards he would earn during his lifetime. He was elected as a Foreign Member of the Royal Society (Great Britain) in 1978 and won the Padma Vibhushan award from the Government of India for distinguished service. Khorana also earned several other awards and accolades in the United States, had several scholarships and awards named after him, and is credited with being one of the founders of the University of Wisconsin's Department of Biochemistry.

- Khorana met his wife, Esther, while he was working at the Swiss Federal Institute of Technology in Zurich. They married in 1952 and had three children.

- While Khorana was working at a lab at the University of British Columbia from 1952 to 1960, he made several breakthroughs in the new field of chemical biology. The research was underfunded, but his work eventually caught the attention of the administration at the University of Wisconsin, who gave him the resources he needed to bring his research to the next level.

- Khorana died November 9, 2011, at the age of 89 at his home in Concord, Massachusetts.

CHAPTER 14

Connie Chung: America's News Anchor

Walter Cronkite was the first true network news anchor in American history, but during the 1980s and 1990s, Connie Chung became the top news anchor for many Americans. For those two decades, Chung led a wave of female reporters, journalists, and news anchors to prominence in what was before that time truly a male-dominated industry, and she was arguably the most visible person of Asian ancestry to do so.

With her warm smile and generally calm demeanor, Chung worked her way into millions of American homes to become a staple of television in that era.

Chung could be found anywhere and everywhere by the late 1990s. She interviewed prominent politicians, heads of state, popular entertainers, and regular people who were newsmakers.

But it wasn't always an easy road for Chung.

She ran into controversy on more than one occasion due to her interview style, which threatened to derail her career. But Chung always seemed to rise above any obstacles and find herself on top. She worked at all of the major networks, did cable news, and hosted several of her own shows.

Chung was the second woman to co-anchor a network weeknight nightly news show, the first to co-anchor the CBS nightly news, and the first person of Asian descent to anchor any show.

IT ALMOST DIDN'T HAPPEN

Connie Chung's career in the media business almost didn't happen because *she* almost didn't happen. Chung was the tenth of ten children, born in 1946 in Maryland to parents who were from China. It was a very different China back then.

China was divided in a civil war from 1927 to 1949 between Mao Zedong's communist forces and Chiang Kai-Shek's nationalist army. Millions of Chinese people died in the fighting and the starvation and disease that happened as a result, including five of Connie's older siblings. As the nationalists were defeated and fled to the island of Formosa (Taiwan), Connie's father, William Linn, also had to flee because he was a diplomat and intelligence officer for the nationalists.

He eventually wound up in the United States where he started over.

William Chung did well for himself and his family in the United States, but he remained traditionally Chinese in many ways until he died. Like all traditional Chinese people, he wanted desperately to have at least one son to carry on his family's name and traditions, but unfortunately, his only sons had died in the Chinese Civil War.

It would basically fall upon Connie to carry on the family's name and honor.

"So, the fact that my father didn't have someone to carry on the Chung name, I really felt I wanted to make the name something," Chung said in a 2011 interview with NPR.

So, Chung did well in school and attended the University of Maryland, earning a degree in journalism in 1969.

Maryland is known for its journalism program and is perfectly situated geographically right in the middle of the Washington, DC media market, so when Chung graduated, she quickly got a job with a local Washington TV station.

Needless to say, there weren't too many women - especially women of Asian descent - doing the news in America in the early 1970s, which had both its positives and negatives for Chung's career trajectory. As she noted in an interview, it was a bit of a cultural taboo for a Chinese female to be an assertive reporter.

"For a small, diminutive-sized Chinese person who grew up in a very loud family and never spoke up in my life, it was dramatic," said Chung, on her decision to go into the news business.

Chung also had to deal with often being the only woman and always being the only person of Asian descent in the newsroom. Although she was never the victim of discrimination or outright hostility, Chung did have to deal with some passive-aggressive attitudes from her colleagues.

"So, I never knew when people were giving me a hard time or understood which reason it was, except when they would say, oh, this is yellow journalism or you slant the news," Chung noted. "I fought it with a sense of humor. I wouldn't let them get my goat by taking it seriously even if they meant it seriously."

Chung's easygoing attitude was a large part of what drove her success. She could joke around with dictators and criminals during interviews in order to produce some really good television, and she was also able to take anything thrown at her if need be.

The diminutive Chinese woman, as she referred to herself, was not a shrinking violet and anyone who stepped into her world quickly learned as much.

Chung's first big interview, and the one that really served as her "big break," took place a little over two years after she graduated from college.

As the Watergate Scandal was just making the news in 1972, Chung was able to land a sit-down interview for CBS with beleaguered President Richard Nixon. The young, attractive Chung used her charm and calm voice to disarm the president before asking him some hard-hitting questions about the scandal. Although Chung wasn't able to get Nixon to admit to anything major, she did score some points with the American people and news executives.

MAKING THE BIG TIME

Chung's success in the Washington market led to offers from all over the country. She eventually took a news anchor job at a Los Angles TV station, which allowed her to raise her profile with another segment of the country and more media executives.

But Chung always wanted to do more. She wanted to reach the pinnacle of her profession, and she could only do that by moving back to the East Coast.

"Oh, yes. I think I had always dreamed of it," Chung said about anchoring a major news show. "I had always dreamt of being Walter Cronkite. You know, all that, you know, Walter, good evening, this is Walter Cronkite. Oh, man. I thought, boy if I could sit in his chair one day. But I always thought it was a dream. I never thought it would really happen. So, when I got to sit in half of his chair, it was a mighty big deal in my mind."

Chung got her first chance to "sit in the chair" when she was the anchor of the *NBC Nightly News* through much of the 1980s. Tom Brokaw and Dan Rather had replaced Walter Cronkite and Eric Sevareid as America's newsmen and anchors, but in the '80s, Connie Chung was well on her way to replacing those guys as America's anchor.

She was bright, warm, and attractive. Chung could also be quite funny when she wanted. In many ways, she was a breath of fresh air from the newsmen and anchors of the past.

And by the late 1980s, all of the networks were after Chung's services!

A fierce bidding war ensued among the major networks when Chung's contract with NBC was up in 1989. She not only stood to gain a financially lucrative contract but also more freedom and exposure. Chung decided to take her talents to CBS, where she made history in 1993 when she co-anchored the *CBS Evening News* with Dan Rather. In doing so, she became only the second woman to co-anchor a network weekly nighttime news show and the first Asian-American.

By 1995, Chung was at the top of the world as her popularity was soaring. In addition to co-anchoring the nightly news, she was also the host of her own news magazine show, *Eye to Eye with Connie Chung*, which mixed hard news interviews with pop culture. But as her star soared in late 1994 and early 1995, the diminutive Chinese American learned just how cutthroat the news business can be.

PROFESSIONAL LANDMINES

Chung quickly found out that, as hard as it was to reach the top of the news business, staying there was an even more herculean task.

The news business is highly competitive to the point of being cutthroat. Aging anchors and reporters are always on guard against up-and-coming talent who likewise are often scheming to move up the ladder.

In late 1994, Chung was one of those upstart talents who had her eye on the top, while Dan Rather was the grey veteran who'd seen it all.

Dan Rather didn't like Chung very much. Chung later admitted as much, stating that his problem with her stemmed from him having to share anchor duties on the nightly news.

"So, when I got to sit in half of his chair, it was a mighty big deal in my mind. I was thrilled. It was difficult for Dan Rather because he had occupied that chair by himself, and to move over a few inches to make room for me or anyone was not an easy thing."

The year 1995 proved to be a high point in many ways for Chung's career, with her landing several high-profile interviews on *Eye to Eye*, but it was also fraught with several professional landmines.

In an interview that was prescient of events today, Chung pressed Bill Gates about the impact Microsoft was having on small businesses across the country. Gates apparently thought he was getting a softball interview from Chung, so when he was faced with some legitimately tough-hitting questions, he walked out of the interview.

Then on January 5, 1995, Speaker of the House of Representatives Newt Gingrich's mother, Kathleen Gingrich, uttered three words that were repeated again and again by reporters and late-night comedians that year - "She's a bitch."

Those were the words Speaker Gingrich's elderly mother quietly muttered when Chung asked her in an *Eye-to-Eye* interview what her son thought of First Lady Hillary Clinton. Trying to be a good Southern woman from an earlier generation, Gingrich at first refused to say anything but finally relented when Chung said, "Just whisper it to me, just between you and me."

Today, Chung would probably be praised, or at least most would've found some humor in the incident, but in 1995, her actions were seen as the worst case of "gotcha journalism" that bordered on trash TV.

Chung survived the maelstrom of negative publicity after the interview, but the storm picked up again months later.

When the Alfred P. Murrah Federal Building was bombed on April 19, 1995, killing 168 people, it was at the time the worst terrorist attack on American soil. Americans were clamoring to find out what happened even as they came together to clear out the wreckage and save as many people as they could. Chung arrived on the scene to interview the rescue workers, asking the Oklahoma City Fire Department spokesman, "Can the Oklahoma City Fire Department handle this?"

Chung emphasized the final word in the question, apparently to stress the level of destruction that had come to Middle America, but most of the people listening at home in Middle America thought the tone was condescending and patronizing.

A major letter-writing campaign to fire Chung began (people still primarily used snail mail at that time), which when combined with Rather's attitude toward her, led to CBS deciding to move Chung to the early mornings and weekends.

It would've been a significant move back for Chung, so she decided to go to ABC in 1998, thereby completing the trifecta of having worked at all three of the major networks of the time. Chung would later go on to work at the Cable News Network (CNN) and ended her TV career on the cable news network MSNBC.

Connie Chung's career in the news business was dramatic, inspiring, and quite volatile at times, yet there's no denying she blazed new trails for women and Americans of Asian ancestry as she became one of the most popular and trusted people in the media during the 1980s and '90s.

DID YOU KNOW?

- Chung married fellow media personality and journalist, Maury Povich, in 1984. Although Povich is best known for his somewhat raunchy *Maury* show, which focuses on paternity tests which reveals more than anything substantive, he was a former reporter and host of the news tabloid show, *A Current Affair*, in the late 1980s. Chung converted to Povich's religion of Judaism after they married and has been an observant Jew since. The couple had an adopted son, Matthew.

- Chung was the first person to interview NBA Hall of Famer Earvin "Magic" Johnson after he announced he was HIV-positive in 1991.

- By 2000, media tastes had changed tremendously with the emergence of the Internet, conservative cable news network Fox News, and talk radio still holding in popularity. Chung's style and even her name were considered old and tired in an every-changing industry.

- Unlike many reporters and even news anchors today, Chung never wore her politics on her sleeve, although her attitudes emerged from time to time. In an interview, Chung once told former tennis great Martina Navratilova that she was unpatriotic for questioning the policies of then-President George W. Bush, stating "Well, you know the old line, love it or leave it."

- In terms of her ethnicity and nationality, Chung says she is as "American as anybody" and thinks of herself as American *and* Chinese but doesn't like the hyphenated label Chinese-American.

CHAPTER 15

Kristi Yamaguchi: Skating Her Way to Victory and into Americans' Hearts

The 1992 Winter Olympics were kind of strange and somewhat forgettable. It wasn't the fault of the athletes who competed in the '92 games in Albertville, France, though.

Their achievements were just overshadowed by some other events.

The breakup of the Soviet Union in 1991, the fall of communism in Europe generally, and the reunification of

Germany were on everyone's minds. The athletes from the former Soviet countries competed as the "Unified Team" under the Olympic flag, and although they did quite well, winning the second top number of medals overall, it just wasn't the same not seeing the USSR flag.

Then there was the timing of the Olympics.

The Olympic Committee decided to have the Winter and Summer Olympics in different years, two years apart from each other, beginning in 1994. This meant that the '92 winter games in Albertville would be followed just two years later by the '94 games in Lillehammer, Norway.

Now, as much as people like watching the Olympics, it's the type of sporting event that people only really like to watch every four years, so when it was announced that another Winter Olympics would take place in 1994, more than a few people tuned out.

The death of Nicolas Bochtay didn't help either.

Bochtay was a Swiss speed skier and was set to compete in the demonstration sport of speed skiing when he was killed in a practice run on February 22, 1992.

So, with all of that drama taking place around the world and at the Olympics, it's no wonder that the '92 Winter Olympics are among the most forgotten by most people. With that said, there were some pretty phenomenal displays of athletic prowess, such as the performance by American figure skater Kristi Yamaguchi.

For many people, Yamaguchi is about all they remember from the Albertville games.

The pretty and graceful 20-year-old caught the attention and won the hearts of Americans and others around the world as she won gold for her country, becoming the first Asian-American woman to win a gold medal in figure skating.

Yamaguchi inspired a generation of girls of all backgrounds and is today one of America's greatest sports heroines.

GETTING HER LEGS

Life for Kristi Yamaguchi began in 1971 in the San Francisco Bay area, and for her, it was a better beginning than what her parents had experienced decades earlier. Kristi's parents, John and Carole, were both Nisei-Americans, but if you remember, that was no help during World War II.

Kristi's grandparents, who were first-generation Japanese-Americans, were sent to an internment camp during the war, which is where Kristi's mother Carole was born. John and Carole Yamaguchi grew up in the shadow of the World War II internment, so they worked hard to build a family and gave Kristi, her brother Brett, and her older sister Lori whatever they could, but also made sure not to spoil them.

John and Carole were both American-born, but they were Nisei so they still held some of the old-world traditions tight, which included pushing their kids.

For the Yamaguchi family academics came first, but extracurricular activities were also important. Lori got into figure skating at an early age and Kristi wanted to follow her, but she had a major obstacle holding her back - she was born with a clubbed foot.

Little Kristi Yamaguchi had a difficult time even walking at age six, never mind doing figure eights in an ice rink, but the Yamaguchi parents were supportive and always looking out for the best interests of their children. After talking to professionals, they learned that athletic training was probably the best thing for Kristi.

So, the Yamaguchi's brought Kristi to skating lessons as a therapy to strengthen her feet and ankles. Before too long, she began enjoying the sport. And she was a natural!

Kristi's combination of natural athletic talent, artistry and good looks made her a top child skater in the Bay area and soon her clubbed foot was history.

Kristi also did ballet to help work past her malady, but by the time she was 12, her life was all about skating. Her rigorous training schedule meant that she had to be homeschooled, which a lot of kids find disappointing, but Yamaguchi didn't mind as long as she got to skate!

And skate she did. By the time she was a teenager, Yamaguchi was winning regional and national competitions and by the late 1980s, she was on the international stage in pairs *and* singles competition.

Competing in pairs and singles figure skating may not sound that big a deal, but it is. It's vastly different from doubles in tennis, where the team is working to score the very concrete and objective goal of points. In figure skating, the athletes perform for judges and in pairs figure skating, everything has to be in sync, *and* the skaters have to look good doing it.

Yamaguchi did well in the pairs competition, winning a bronze medal in the 1987 World Junior Championships and a gold medal in the 1988 World Junior Championships, which was in addition to the gold she won in the singles competition of the '88 World Junior Championships.

But Yamaguchi knew that she had to pick one or the other, so she decided to go on her own.

KRISTI, NANCY, AND TANYA

Yamaguchi was a successful pairs skater right up until the time she left it behind in 1990. She and partner Rudy Galindo had won numerous national and international competitions, but the graceful Yamaguchi had to have a stage of her own. After winning gold at the 1990 Goodwill Games in singles competition, Yamaguchi knew she had made the right choice.

But as much of a natural Yamaguchi was on the ice, there were still a few more bumps in the road she'd encounter.

Before 1991, Yamaguchi may have looked and performed like an adult on the ice, but she was still very much a young girl off the ice. After wowing crowds with her performance to "Madame Butterfly," the teen Yamaguchi had a difficult time dealing with reporters and fans. She giggled quite a bit and gave one-word, yes or no answers to most questions, which led to some criticism.

So, she and her family knew that things had to change a bit. Beginning in 1991, Yamaguchi decided to train in Canada with coach Christy Ness. Yamaguchi focused on her training, but she also took classes at the University of Alberta and matured into adulthood. She never lost the smile that won the hearts of so many of her fans, but she became more articulate and media savvy.

She also made the difficult decision to end her partnership with Galindo and leave pairs skating in the past.

"Last year definitely had a positive effect," Yamaguchi said to an *LA Times* reporter in 1992, just before the Winter Olympics. "I concentrated on singles at my competitions and put in all of my energy that went before into two practices a day. I know it would have been difficult if I had two other events to worry about at the world championships."

Yamaguchi's hard work in Canada and concentration on singles competition immediately began paying dividends as she came in second at the 1991 US Figure Skating Championships in February 1991 and won the 1991 World Figure Skating Championships in March 1991 in Munich, Germany.

She placed second at the US Championships to Tonya Harding and just ahead of Harding and Nancy Kerrigan at the World Championships.

Yes, that Harding and Kerrigan.

Since this story is about Kristi Yamaguchi and her role as a genuine Asian-American heroine, I don't want to spend too much time on the whole Harding-Kerrigan rivalry, but Yamaguchi did play a peripheral role in it. And as mentioned earlier, the events that happened in 1994 in many ways, unfortunately, overshadowed Yamaguchi's accomplishment of winning gold in 1992.

So, let's talk a bit about it.

You now know that Yamaguchi, Harding, and Kerrigan were the top three ladies figure skaters for Team USA going into the 1992 Winter Olympics. They very well could have swept the medals as they had at the 1991 World Championships.

You also probably know that Harding, or at least people associated with her, paid someone to injure Kerrigan before the 1994 competition. Although the attack failed and Kerrigan went on to win silver in the 1994 Winter Olympics and Harding went home empty-handed, the talk everywhere was about the attack on Kerrigan.

But in 1992, everything was cool between the three girls, at least according to a 2018 interview Yamaguchi gave.

"We all had a fairly good relationship," Yamaguchi noted about the three women.

So, luckily for Yamaguchi, in 1992, she only had to beat her opponents on the ice in France - there were no paid thugs for her to overcome!

WINNING THE GOLD

Yamaguchi may not have had thugs with clubs to deal with as Kerrigan did in 1994, she did face some pretty stiff competition on the ice.

Although Yamaguchi was - and still is - quite athletic, her athleticism was of a different type to Harding's or Japanese skater Midori Ito's.

Ito was the first female figure skater to land a triple-triple jump combination and a triple axel in competition, and Harding's raw strength could be quite intimidating to the other women in the competition.

So, Yamaguchi fell back on her training as a ballerina and performed a routine that relied on choreography and being technically sound. After winning the gold in 1992, Yamaguchi returned back to the States as a sort of conquering hero. She was placed on the pedestal of American figure skating history with Dorothy Hamill and Peggy Fleming and every little girl figure skater tried to emulate Yamaguchi's gold medal-winning routine.

America truly fell in love with Kristi Yamaguchi and among them, many Asian-Americans, especially girls, began to see her as a true heroine. For Yamaguchi, she didn't really think about what her success meant to other Asian-Americans until she got home and let everything sink in.

"I was just one generation away from my family who lost everything and had to rebuild their entire lives and improve their loyalty to this country," Yamaguchi said in a 2018 interview. "So, that's when I realized, 'Oh, wow. Yes, I'm able to live out the American dream because of the work and the sacrifices of the generations before me.'"

Yamaguchi went professional after the 1992 season, but stayed active in the sport, skating with the Stars on Ice and in professional competitions for most of the 1990s.

DID YOU KNOW?

- Yamaguchi married former NHL player Bret Hedican in 2000. They had two daughters and live together in Northern California. Yamaguchi was actually introduced to Hedican by Nancy Kerrigan.

- When asked about Harding in the 1992 *LA Times* interview just before the Olympics, Yamaguchi said: "I don't think there's a rivalry between us, or between Tonya and me. I believe it's just the skating that matters."

- Yamaguchi skated with fellow American gold medalist, Scott Hamilton, in the opening ceremonies of the 2002 Winter Olympics in Salt Lake City, Utah.

- Yamaguchi was inducted into the U.S. Figure Skating Hall of Fame in 1998 and the World Figure Skating Hall of Fame in 1999.

- In addition to her skating career, Yamaguchi has also done some acting, appearing in small roles in several films and TV shows, and has also authored a children's book titled *Dream Big, Little Pig!*

CHAPTER 16

Hiram Fong: Hawaii's First Senator

When Hawaii became the US' 50th state in 1959, most Americans really didn't know what to think; the vast majority of Americans had never been there. It was a couple of decades before air travel became common and affordable, and Hawaii had yet to really become the tourist hotspot it is today. For most Americans, Hawaii was a very exotic place, full of exotic people who weren't traditionally considered Americans.

It was a place, in many Americans' eyes, where Americans would only visit if they were somehow connected to the military.

But Hawaii was very much a part of America in 1959, and as we saw earlier in this book, it had been for some time. Hawaii's grafting into the American union wasn't always easy and it followed a different course than the rest of the country in many ways.

Similar to the continental US, Hawaii had an indigenous population that was conquered by American political, economic, and military powers, not to mention sheer numbers, but that's where the similarities end.

Since Hawaii was so far away from the rest of the country, it remained relatively "Hawaiian" in its culture and most of the immigrants who settled there were from China and Japan. The majority of the generational Americans who moved to Hawaii were businesspeople or in the military, which is the case even today.

So, when Hawaii became a state in 1959, and it was allotted two senators and an at-large congressman per the US Constitution, the people of the new state sent representatives with their ethnic backgrounds to Washington.

Japanese American Daniel Inouye became Hawaii's first US congressman, although Dalip Saund (remember him?), beat him out in the honor to become the first Asian-American to serve in congress.

Due to the Constitution requiring two senators from every state no matter the population, Hawaii sent two senators to Washington that year. The first was long-time Democratic politician Oren Long. Long was an Anglo- American who had served for years in Hawaii's territorial senate.

The second senator from Hawaii proved to be a true barrier breaker and a bit of an anomaly - Hiram Fong. Fong was born and raised in Hawaii, and like Long, served for years in the Hawaiian territorial congress before being elected to the US Senate.

A longtime advocate of Hawaiian statehood, Fong became the nation's first Asian-American senator, Hawaii's only Republican senator, and the first Asian-American to be a serious candidate for president.

Thanks to Hiram Fong, Hawaii's profile was raised, and by the time he retired from the Senate in 1977, the Aloha state was a little more American but still unique and exotic.

GROWING UP HAWAIIAN AND AMERICAN

In 1872, as thousands of Chinese left their homeland for the United States to work in the gold and silver mines of the West and to help build the Transcontinental Railroad when his ship stopped over in Oahu, Fong Sau Howe decided to stay in the Kingdom of Hawaii (remember, it was an independent country at that time). Fong worked in the sugar fields of Oahu and eventually met and married Lum Shee, another Chinese immigrant.

The Fong family was poor and illiterate, but proud. The Fongs had 11 children, the seventh of which was Ah Leong, who later changed his name to "Hiram."

Hiram grew up fast in the Kalihi neighborhood of Honolulu.

Since his parents were far from the "Crazy Rich Asians" of recent movie fame, young Hiram had to learn how to earn an honest living at a young age. He began working at the tender age of four by picking beans, and eventually landed a better-paying job as a shipyard clerk during his teens.

Fong worked long hours and often missed school due to work or sleep, but he still did well in school. Although his parents didn't have personal experience with formal education, and they didn't speak English, they were generally supportive of his quest for an education.

After Fong graduated from high school in 1924, he was accepted to the University of Hawaii, where he was transformed from just another poor Chinese kid into a genuine intellectual.

In addition to a full course load, Fong took part in many extra-curricular activities. He was an editor for the school's newspaper, *Ka Leo*, and the university's yearbook. Fong's editing activities helped prepare him for his later legal and political careers, where regular writing was a mainstay.

Fong also joined the university's debate team, where he honed his speaking skills, made contact with a number of Hawaii's future business and political leaders, and came out of his shell.

Fong demonstrated his patriotism as an American citizen by joining the Reserve Officer Training Corp (ROTC) at the University of Hawaii, which would later put him on track to be an officer in the United States Army during World War II.

But Fong's true talents were his writing and speaking abilities and by the late 1920s, it was clear his future would probably be in law or politics, or both.

Fong got his first taste of political life when he wrote and delivered speeches for Honolulu's sheriff candidate, Patrick K. Gleason. Many in Hawaii's political circles were impressed with the young Chinese American, especially since few Chinese people were involved in Hawaii's political scene. At that time - and still today, to a certain extent - politics in Hawaii were controlled by those of Japanese descent and White people.

So, many were intrigued with the young Fong, especially Fred Wright, who invited Fong to help him with his successful campaign to become Honolulu's mayor in 1931.

As Fong worked with Wright, he continued with his education and eventually graduated with honors from Hawaii in 1930, but it was just the beginning of his journey.

"YOU CAN'T GO WRONG WITH FONG"

After Fong graduated from college, he had several options open to him. He had offers to go into business with some friends that he'd made, and he could've entered politics at that time. Instead, he chose to work for the Suburban Water System of Oahu for two years before going on to law school.

Fong was accepted to the prestigious Harvard Law School, where he was subjected to a healthy dose of culture shock. It was the first time Fong had been in the continental US, and Massachusetts' cold winters, intense people, and urban sprawl were nothing like he was used to in Hawaii. Not to mention, he was one of only a few students of Asian descent in a student body of primarily East Coast WASPs and Jews.

But Fong did like he always did by keeping his nose in the books and graduating with a JD in 1935. With the Great Depression ravaging most of the world, Fong wanted nothing more than to go back to his home in Hawaii and be around his family and familiar territory, so he went back to Honolulu to practice law.

When Fong moved back home, things moved fast. He got married, started a family, and after working for the prosecutor's office in Honolulu, founded a private law firm: Fong, Miho, Choy, and Robinson. The firm was a reflection of Hawaiian society in many ways with the partners being Chinese (Fong), Japanese (Miho), Korean (Choy), and native Hawaiian and white (Robinson).

But while Fong worked in the legal profession, he longed to be in politics. Politics was his true calling, so in 1938, he ran for and won a seat in Hawaii's territorial legislature. Fong would go on to serve in the territorial legislature for 14 years, minus a brief period when he served as a judge advocate in World War II.

By 1945, Fong was a notable political leader and a vocal advocate of Hawaiian statehood. Fong was born an American citizen and believed that despite its cultural uniqueness, Hawaii had earned the right to become a state.

So, when Congress passed and President Dwight D. Eisenhower signed into law, the Hawaii Admission Act on March 18, 1959, the people of the new state of Hawaii would need to choose one congressman and two senators (the House is chosen by population, while every state, no matter the size, gets two senators). This was Fong's chance to realize his lifelong ambition, but he had just one problem - he was a Republican!

Hawaii is today and always has been a strong Democrat state. Long before California was the liberal utopian's dream, Hawaii was that place. So, for Fong to win a statewide election in liberal Hawaii, he needed to run a great campaign and build a strong base.

As far as building a base, he had already done that beginning with his time in college and continuing through his service in the territorial legislature. Fong was able to build a coalition that crossed ethnic lines and included labor as well as some of the leading businessmen in Hawaii at the time.

Running a great campaign, though, was easier said than done, especially since he had a tough opponent.

Fong's opponent was Frank Fasi, who was one of Hawaii's territorial senators and who would later serve as the mayor of Honolulu for 22 years. Fasi was definitely a tough opponent and a Democrat, but Fong ran an energetic, positive, and modern campaign that pushed him through to victory.

As Fong's supporters said, "You Can't Go Wrong with Fong!"

Fong won the election and immediately became a popular, independent representative of Hawaii. Fong served as senator of Hawaii until he retired in 1976 after tiring from the hectic schedule and travel. He was also popular within the national Republican Party. In 1964, he even received five delegates for the party's presidential nomination at the party's convention in Daly City, California.

A major part of Fong's independent nature was his ability to cross party lines and work with Democrats. Perhaps part of that was the result of him coming from a state dominated by the Democrats, while his ethnic background also played a role.

Fong voted for civil rights legislation and to end restrictive immigration laws, but he also supported US military involvement in Southeast Asia and was a major supporter of President Richard Nixon.

Through it all, Fong voted with his conscience and did what he thought was best for the state of Hawaii.

Later Hawaii politicians of Asian ancestry recognized Fong as a trailblazer to whom they owed a debt of gratitude.

"I think what he did was that he kept the door open here in Hawai'i for those of us of Asian descent to reach higher," former Hawaii congressman Pat Saiki said after Fong died in 2004.

DID YOU KNOW?

- After retiring from politics, Fong returned to Hawaii to help run his family business comprising insurance, real estate, and investing. Despite the businesses being successful for most of Fong's life, one of his sons sued him, forcing Fong and his wife to declare bankruptcy in 2003.

- Fong was a devout member of the Congregationalist Church. He chose the name "Hiram" in honor of Hiram Bingham, a 19th-century Congregationalist who brought the church's message to Hawaii.

- One of Fong's post-Senate commercial ventures was "Senator Fong's Plantation and Gardens," which was a 725-acre commercial botanical garden.

- Fong married fellow Chinese- American and Hawaiian, Ellyn Lo, in 1938. The couple had four children.

- During his time in the Senate, Fong served on several committees. He was the highest-ranking Republican on the Post Office and Civil Service Committee and was also on the Appropriations Committee, the Judiciary Committee, and the Special Committee on Aging. His tenure in the Senate came under full or partial terms of four presidents: Kennedy (D), Johnson (D), Nixon (R), and Ford (R).

CHAPTER 17

Henry Cho: Asian Humor with a Touch of Country

Or maybe it's country humor with a touch of Asian!

Well, if you've ever heard one of the standup routines of Korean American comedian Henry Cho, you know what I mean. Since Cho made a splash with his unique brand of observational humor in the 1980s, he has carved out a niche in the entertainment for himself as the "Asian guy with the southern accent."

And he was certainly a sight when he first hit the stage in those early years.

Often wearing cowboy boots, occasionally wearing a bolo tie, and usually with a mullet haircut (at least until the early '90s), Cho was a comedian that his primarily white audiences had never seen - and had never heard before in their lives, as he also became known for his thick, often overdone east Tennessee accent and probably never would again!

But Cho proved he was much more than a gimmick. For more than 30 years, Cho has amused countless people with stories of growing up Asian-American in East Tennessee, and he's done so on his own terms – clean humor.

In addition to being one of the better-known Asian-American comedians today, Henry Cho is what's known as a "clean" comedian, doing family-friendly acts. Today, Cho is one of the top performers on the Christian standup comedy circuit and has appeared in film, television, and commercials, while building a sizable following of loyal fans.

And like the other heroes and heroines in this book, Cho was a real trailblazer. Following in the footsteps of Pat Morita, Henry Cho opened the door for other Korean- American comedians, such as Margaret Cho (no relation) and Ken Jeon, and for that, he is a true Asian-American hero.

GROWING UP SOUTHERN, AND KOREAN

If you're familiar with the American South at all, you know that just like the rest of the United States, it has its own unique regional culture. As friendly as Southerners are, they're often leery of outsiders, especially outsiders who look and sound a little different from the locals.

This was the culture Henry Cho was born into in 1962 in Knoxville, Tennessee.

Cho's parents were Korean immigrants, who worked him to give him a good home and as with many Asian immigrants, did what they could so Henry could assimilate and be part of the community.

And for the most part, the Cho's were successful. Henry did well in school, had plenty of friends, and never got into trouble. Young Henry enjoyed Southern cooking like grits and barbeque, was a fan of country music and was and still is a huge fan of college football.

But he was regularly reminded of his Korean ancestry.

As Cho has pointed out in some of his standup routines, locals often asked him if he knew the Chinese family running the local laundry and was sometimes told to "drop by and see" various other Asian residents of Knoxville.

Cho got along reasonably well with the other kids in his neighborhood, but as he noted in some of his comedy routines, it was clear he was different.

"Guys, you guys remember playing army as a kid?" Cho asked in routine at the Improv in Los Angeles, California. "You pretty much guessed it; I hated this game. All my buddies would go, okay Henry, it's the neighborhood against you." He then added that when they played cowboys and Indians, "I was always the cook."

But instead of dwelling on things, Cho developed a sense of humor about the situation and when combined with his keen insight and intellect, he was able to find humor in his parents' Korean background, the Southern background of his neighbors and friends, and his own background that shared the two cultures.

Cho's journey to be an A-list professional standup comedian didn't happen overnight, although he did want to do standup at a young age. As a child, he began writing down many of his experiences, and he also listened to Bob Newhart and Bill Cosby standup records (yes, that was the primary medium in the '70s) in his spare time.

It was comedians such as those standup guys, who influenced Cho's clean style.

But after Cho graduated high school and attended the University of Tennessee in Knoxville, he never dreamed that in less than ten years he'd be opening for Jerry Seinfeld in some of the biggest comedy clubs in the US.

KEEPING IT CLEAN

Tennessee is part of the "Bible Belt," where churches are as common as pick-up trucks and hunting dogs. So, Cho grew up immersed in that environment and it became a core part of his belief system and would play a major role in how he did his comedy. While in college, Cho was a leader in the Christian Young Life organization, and as much as his faith was, and still is, important to him, he could still find humor in those who were more risqué in the comedy world.

Still, when Cho decided to make the big step by entering an open comedy competition in Knoxville in 1986, he kept things clean.

He won the competition, got a contract to tour the region, and the rest, as they say, is history.

Well, not quite. Cho may have been a hit in the southeast, but if he was ever going to make it real big, he knew he had to bring his special type of clean comedy to the belly of the beast -Hollywood.

After Cho arrived in Hollywood, he was under immense pressure to make his act "blue" by adding some swear words and maybe a couple of lewd stories. But that wasn't Henry Cho, and thankfully, he received some advice from a pretty successful comedian to keep true to his style.

"Shortly after I got into comedy, I worked with Jerry Seinfeld. I got the gig since I was the only clean opener within miles," said Cho in a 2013 interview about his decision to keep his act clean. "Jerry told me to keep working clean for professional reasons, if you can't do a joke on television why spend time on it. He was great and took me on the road with him for several gigs. I learned from the best."

And being himself truly proved to be the formula for success for Henry Cho.

"Just let it soak in a second or two cause there's something wrong with this picture ain't there?" Cho opened one of his early acts at the Improv in Los Angeles wearing cowboy boots and a mullet. "You're kinda going - hang on there's an Oriental up there talking like a hillbilly. And I know this ain't quite right but you'll get used to it, I swear."

By the early 1990s, Cho was headlining performances, doing sets on all the major late-night talk shows, and began appearing in film and TV, such as the 1992 made-for-TV movie *Revenge of the Nerds III: The Next Generation*, where the native Tennessean appropriately played a "South" Korean Elvis impersonator.

Today, Cho writes for television and continues to act but lives full-time in his home state of Tennessee. Cho's journey from obscurity to success is a testament to his tenacity and he stands as a rare sort of trailblazer that proves you can't always judge a book by its cover.

DID YOU KNOW?

- Although Cho's faith is a major part of his life and career, and he's even turned down film roles over it, he's no prude. He admits that one of his favorite comedians is the often raucous Chris Rock.

- Cho has performed several times at the iconic Grand Ole Opry in Nashville, Tennessee, which puts him into a small group with such music legends as Johnny Cash, Patsy Cline, and Elvis Presley, and an even smaller one since he is one of the few Asians to have performed at the historic theater.

- Cho married his wife, Amy, in 1998. The couple have three children and are still married and living in Nashville.

- Cho has performed and acted consistently since the 1980s, but his career had a second success spike in the early to mid-2000s when blue-collar/rural humor became popular with the likes of Jeff Foxworthy, Larry the Cable Guy, and Bill Engvall. The popularity of the genre led to Cho getting his own show on the Comedy Central network in 2006 titled, *Henry Cho: What's That Clickin' Noise?*

- With the advent of the internet, Cho got on board but unfortunately found out that henrycho.com was taken by a Taekwondo master. Cho joked, "Unfortunately, .com was taken by the karate guy S. Henry, on everything else except his site. Told me he used my name to get more hits.

He's right, but what do you do, call a 7th-degree black belt out into the street? The sad thing is I've asked him a few times to let me at least put an icon on his site, you know, Henry Cho-Comedian. He's not let me up to this date."

CHAPTER 18

The 442nd Infantry Regiment: Fighting Two Wars at the Same Time

In numerous chapters of this book, we've detailed how some of our Japanese-Americans heroes' and heroines' stories began in the American internment camps during World War II. And make no mistake about it, these *were* concentration camps by any definition. Nearly all people of Japanese ancestry living on the West Coast when Pearl Harbor was attacked were sent to these camps, and although the conditions in them were not as terrible as concentration camps in Germany or earlier in South Africa, they were concentration camps nonetheless.

Those of Japanese ancestry, even American citizens, lost all their civil liberties in the name of national security and they were left with the label of being disloyal.

By the 1980s, even the fairly conservative US government agreed that those of Japanese ancestry had been mistreated during World War II and deserved an official apology and monetary compensation to the survivors. This was all covered by the Civil Liberties Act of 1988, which President Ronald Reagan signed into law.

The signing of the act seemed to have righted a wrong that most today see as a dark period of American history.

But as with most things, the situation wasn't always so black and white.

Not all Japanese Americans were sent to the internment camps. Those outside the West Coast - for instance, those in New York City - remained free, for the most part, unless they were new arrivals or were thought to have pro-Japan sympathies. And as we saw earlier with Wally Yonamine and his family, most of the Japanese in Hawaii were also left alone.

But the Japanese in Hawaii didn't totally avoid suspicion and discrimination during the war.

After the Pearl Harbor attack, the predominantly Nisei Hawaii Territorial guard prepared to report to duty but were told their services were no longer needed and to turn in their weapons. The governor of Hawaii also discharged all Nisei and students of Japanese ancestry from the University of Hawaii's ROTC program.

So how did the Nisei respond?

They responded by forming a volunteer civilian group known as the Varsity Victory Battalion, which helped the American war effort by building roads and military installations.

But many of the Nisei, despite what they had been through, still wanted to fight.

The Army eventually reformed the predominantly Nisei 298th and 299th Hawaii National Guard battalions and sent them to the mainland, where they became the 100th Infantry Battalion. There, the more than 1,300 men of the 100th would form the core of the new all-Nisei 442nd Infantry Regiment. In addition to the Nisei Hawaiians of the 100th, many of the men of the 442nd came straight from the internment camps.

Some joined the 442nd as a legal way to escape the camps, but others joined out of genuine patriotism. Yes, even after losing everything due to President Roosevelt's executive order, the men of the 442nd made the courageous choice to serve their country and to essentially fight two wars: one on the battlefield against their country's enemies and the other at home against their government's policies and attitudes.

PATRIOTIC NISEI

When the 298th and 299th regiments were sent to Fort McCoy, Wisconsin to begin their official training as members of the US Army in June 1942, most people didn't know what to expect. The Army wanted to move the Nisei soldiers far from the West Coast and never planned to use them for fighting in the Pacific as the government still questioned their loyalties. The 100th would be trained in the middle of Wisconsin, which is, of course, in the middle of America.

Sending the 100th to Fort McCoy, though, was a little ironic, or possibly cynical. In addition to its being a standard Army base, Fort McCoy also functioned as a concentration camp, where 170 Japanese-Americans and 120 German-American and Italian-American citizens deemed disloyal were being held.

For many of the soldiers of the 100th, it was the first they'd seen America outside of Hawaii. Many had never seen snow before and few had experienced the frigid winter they lived through in 1942-1943.

Although all of the 100th's officers were white, often with degrees in psychology to check members for their perceived loyalty, they gave the Nisei soldiers a certain amount of freedom. The Army decided to treat them more or less like the other units, so the 100th formed their own baseball and other sports teams to compete against the white units.

Five members of the 100th even rescued some local residents who fell through the ice of a nearby lake.

But the Nisei soldiers weren't there to see dairy farms or internees, they were there to train to make up the bulk of the 442nd Army Regiment.

In January 1943, the War Department directed that the 442nd Army Regiment would be comprised of American men of Japanese ancestry. Although the order allowed all men of Japanese ancestry who were *born* in the US to join (remember back to Dalip Saund, Asians weren't allowed to become naturalized citizens until after World War II), the overwhelming majority who fitted the requirements were Nisei.

The 100th shipped out to Camp Shelby, Mississippi to join 3,000 more volunteers from Hawaii and another 800 from the mainland to officially make up the 442nd Regiment.

Since the 100th had received training before the other battalions of the 442nd, and since most of its members were experienced National Guardsmen, they were sent to North Africa first, landing there on September 2, 1943.

But once more the 100th was forced to prove itself.

The 100th actually had to "offer" to fight under General and future American President Dwight D. Eisenhower, but he refused to accept them. After some back-and-forth with his generals, General Mark Clark agreed to graft the 100th to the 34th Infantry Division until the 442nd completed their training and entered the theater of battle.

You see, the military was highly segregated by race at that time, so in addition to Eisenhower not trusting or believing the 100th could fight, their inclusion with white units went against the military policy of the period.

But beginning in September 1943, the 100th was engaged in several battles in the fight for Italy, distinguishing itself every time.

By the time the 442nd arrived in Europe by the summer of 1944, the 100th was an experienced combat unit that had earned the respect of many of its fellow Americans, and its foes on the other side alike.

"GO FOR BROKE"

When the 442nd arrived in Europe, their fellow Nisei of the 100th were already battle-hardened veterans who had earned the respect of their fellow Americans. The 100th particularly distinguished itself in the long, hard-fought Battle of Monte Cassino in Italy from January 17 to May 18, 1944.

The Battle of Monte Cassino was Germany's last major defensive stand in Italy, as around 150,000 German soldiers dug in fortifications that stretched across the central peninsula in what they called the "Gustav Line."

The assault on the Gustav Line was fierce, and the Allies took a lot of casualties, but the men of the 100th were up to the task, nearly taking several strategic objectives.

The Allies incurred more than 55,000 casualties, with the 100th being reduced from 1,300 men to just 500. Because of their efforts at the Battle of Monte Cassino, the 100th earned the nickname "the purple heart battalion", and the men developed a genuine *esprit de corps.*

The 100th developed the motto "Go for Broke" to symbolize all they believed in and how they fought, and wanted to be remembered, on the battlefield. When the rest of the 442nd joined the 100th in Italy in the summer of 1944, they also adopted the slogan as well as the general attitude and style of the veteran combat unit.

After fighting in Italy, the 442nd worked its way into southern France where it engaged the Germans in numerous battles, the most famous of which was the rescue of the "Lost Battalion."

GENERAL DAHLQUIST AND THE LOST BATTALION

General John Dahlquist was the type of man any commander would want to keep things in order. The Swedish-American general from Minnesota was brought up in a culture of order and tidiness and some would say it was in his DNA, but the good organization behind the front doesn't always translate to great leadership in battle.

Dahlquist commanded the 36th Infantry Division, to which the 442nd was later attached.

Dahlquist, who had no combat experience before World War II, was accused of making poor battlefield decisions in general and was particularly criticized for using the 442nd as cannon fodder as they worked their way through France.

But Dahlquist wasn't liberal with only the lives of his Japanese-American soldiers.

On October 24, 1944, Dahlquist ordered the 1st Battalion of the 141st Infantry to attack a heavily fortified German position in the Vosges Mountains on the France-Germany border. The Americans were quickly surrounded and within hours 275 soldiers were trapped in a state of siege that lasted nearly a week.

Supplies were airdropped to the 1st Battalion, but it was the men of the 442nd who eventually fought their way in and out of the position.

The 442nd achieved their goal by bringing the surrounded Americans out of the mountains, but 161 of them were killed.

After the big victory of saving the Lost Battalion, there was no time to rest for the 442nd. They were engaged in action in southern France and then returned to Italy to close out the war in Europe in May 1945.

When the war in Europe ended, the 442nd returned to Hawaii where it was de-activated in 1947. The America that the men of the 442nd returned to after the war was very different though. It would be decades before the US government formally apologized for the internment of American citizens of Japanese descent, the accomplishments of the 442nd, and particularly the 100th Battalion, were commemorated by the Army, historians, and Japanese Americans in the years immediately after they returned home.

DID YOU KNOW?

- In addition to "Go for Broke," the 100th's motto was "Remember Pearl Harbor." The official fight song of the 442nd started with the line, "Remember Pearl Harbor."

- Although 21 soldiers of the 442nd earned the coveted Medal of Army for heroic actions during the war, most of them were awarded the medals later in their lives or posthumously. One of the few Medal of Honor awards given just after the war to a Japanese-American was to Private First Class Sadao Munemori. Munemori was a Nisei from Los Angeles who enlisted in the Army before Pearl Harbor. After the 442nd formed, he was one of its first mainland recruits, training with the unit and traveling with them to Italy where he died on April 5, 1945, when he jumped on a live grenade to save two of his comrades.

- By the 1950s the attitude toward Japanese people, and Asians in general, had changed quite a bit in the US. The Cold War was the major conflict in the world at the time, so the Russians became the primary "bad guy" in American policy, and many Asian peoples, such as the Japanese, were seen as more virtuous in their stand against communism. The 1951 American film *Go For Broke!* is a bit of a reflection of that Cold War attitude. The film was a fictional portrayal of the 442nd's history, portraying the Nisei as brave, freedom-loving Americans.

- Although all the men of the 442nd were in the same situation of having to fight attitudes at home as well as enemies overseas, they had quite a rivalry among themselves. The mainland Nisei, who considered themselves more street smart and truly American, referred to the Hawaiian Nisei as "Buddhaheads." The origin of this term is unknown, although it may come from "butahead" (pig-head, possibly referring to the preferred meat on Hawaii), or it may have to do with a more recent slang term for the head of a family. Not wanting to be outdone, the Hawaiians referred to the mainland Nisei as "katonks." The origin of katonk is also unknown, but Hawaiian Nisei said it was the sound their heads made after hitting the floor.

- Among the best-known veterans of the 442nd was Hawaii Senator Daniel Inouye (1924-2012).

CONCLUSION

I hope you enjoyed reading The Great Book of Asian-American Heroes: 18 Asian-American Men and Women Who Have Influenced American History and had a little fun as you learned a thing or two about the contributions and sacrifices Asian-Americans have made to and for American history and culture. Before reading this, you probably knew that heroes and heroines come from many different backgrounds and experiences, and after reading this book, you now know that within the ethnic group designated Asian-American, the heroes and heroines come from many different backgrounds and have had a diverse range of experiences that brought them to hero or heroine status.

Many of the heroes and heroines in this book had to deal with official discrimination in the form of the government, as was the case with Japanese-Americans in World War II, but some, such as Iwao Takamoto used the experience to better themselves, while others, like Pat Morita, learned how to deal with it with humor.

You learned about Asian-American trailblazers in the American government, like Dalip Saund and Hiram Fong, who ran for office at a time when it was unheard of for most Asians to vote, never mind hold office.

You also learned that there have been some pretty phenomenal Asian athletes - such as Bruce Lee, Wally Yonamine, and Kristi Yamaguchi - who successfully challenged the stereotype of Asians being only bookish and not very athletic.

Finally, all of the heroes and heroines in our book provide a great template for anyone, of any ethnicity, who is striving to overcome adversity. All of our heroes and heroines overcame incredible obstacles to reach the top of their professions, whether in sports, entertainment, politics, art, or science. All of these men and women are to be admired for what they've done and the role they've played in uplifting their respective communities and by proving that they too are Americans who are more than capable of contributing to the American experience.

Made in the USA
Monee, IL
25 February 2022

91805881R00105